KONSTANTIN KOZHEVNIKOV

YOU CAN

BECOME YOUR OWN BEST FRIEND AND BE HAPPY, HEALTHY AND WEALTHY

МОГУ СТАТЬ СВОИМ ЛУЧШИМ ДРУГОМ
И ЖИТЬ СВОБОДНО И СЧАСТЛИВО

EDITOR XENIA KOZHEVNIKOVA

GALATI

2024

YOU CAN. BECOME YOUR OWN BEST FRIEND AND BE HAPPY, HEALTHY AND WEALTHY / Konstantin Kozhevnikov. — 2024. — 256 p.

ISBN 978-973-0-40983-3

How to achieve success, tackle life's complex challenges, and build wealth? How to build and sustain harmonious family relationships for nearly 40 years? How to, in spite of a busy schedule, spend a quarter of a century being a present and engaged father? How to become more energetic with age and truly enjoy life?

This book offers clear and straightforward insights into these profound questions — without any 'magic pills,' just real, proven strategies and the valuable experiences of the author who has invested millions in mastering them.

In addition, the book provides lessons in strategic thinking and ten rules for a happy life, specifically for those who have yet to find success or are unsure where to begin.

Konstantin Kozhevnikov — entrepreneur, mentor, public figure, and leader with 35 years of experience as a professional problem solver in various fields, industries, companies, banks, and organizations — shares his practical experiences of both victories and defeats, discussing effective methods of achieving goals.

This book is designed to help readers build their own frameworks for happiness, success, freedom, and balance.

Throughout my career as a real estate coach, I've learned that personal development is just as essential as professional growth. Konstantin's book presents a refreshing and effective way to nurture both. It encourages readers to build a solid foundation for success by becoming their own best supporter and creating a mindset that thrives under pressure.

The principles and strategies laid out in this book resonate deeply with anyone striving to balance career ambitions with personal fulfillment. Instead of simply focusing on financial achievement, Konstantin emphasizes a holistic approach that integrates mental well-being and self-awareness as key components of success.

If you're committed to improving yourself and seeking a comprehensive guide to achieving happiness, health, and professional success, then this book is exactly what you need.

Eric Orland,
Real Estate Coach and Founder of Attraction Flow, LLC,
Industry Veteran and Top-Producing Agent

Golf teaches us that we cannot always be perfect, that we need to focus on the process, and that the path to perfection is discipline and practice. Much of this is applicable to our everyday lives. This book is an excellent find for anyone, like me, who constantly strives for happiness, fulfillment, and self-realization.

Victoria Pertierra Monforte,
Multiple World, European, Spanish, and International Golf Champion

It's common to talk a lot about happiness, but happiness is a space for reflections even more vast than space itself.

This book helps to piece together precisely that more complete puzzle describing happiness.

Yuri Malenchenko,
Pilot-Cosmonaut, Completed 6 Spaceflights
and Ranks Second in the World
for Total Time Spent in Orbit (827 Days)

When you read this book, believe me, many times you'll want to exclaim, 'Darn, that's right! That's exactly it! I've experienced that too!'

Nikolai Fomenko,
Film Actor, TV and Radio Presenter

As a former professional golfer who has played on both the PGA Tour and European Tour, and as a coach who has trained local sporting icons, celebrities, and international stars, I know that achieving success requires not just physical training but also the right mental attitude. Konstantin's book serves as a powerful reminder that the most important ally on the road to success is ourselves.
This book provides practical advice and techniques to help find balance between work, personal life, and mental well-being. Konstantin shares his own experiences and shows how to become your own best friend, take care of your inner world, and learn valuable lessons from challenging situations.
I highly recommend this book to anyone striving for success who wants to learn how to support themselves on the path to happiness, health, and prosperity.

Don Gammon,
Former PGA Tour and European Tour Golfer,
Coach to South African and International Stars

Deep, insightful book. It feels like it's been forged through experience, yet it reads easily, accessibly, with wisdom packaged in a very comprehensible and therefore attractive manner. The main thing it managed to avoid is, on the one hand, moralizing, and on the other hand, the book is absolutely unlike endless business motivators and the hype about 'successful success'.

Kirill Kiknadze,
Journalist, TV Presenter, Filmmaker, and Program Author

From the earliest childhood, I've realized how incredibly lucky I am. In my life, there is a father who is ready not only to pass on his knowledge and experience, but also to delve deeply into my questions and problems, without devaluing my own feelings and sensations, so that, having listened, he could genuinely give advice that would change the situation for the better. I always knew and know that I can rely on him as like a good friend. But as growing up, I realized something - this 'friend' has been me all this time. He managed to reflect my thoughts, emotions, and values back to me in a way that made me a better person. This is a superpower possessed by my dad, and I'm genuinely happy that he decided to encapsulate it in a tangible object that I can place on my bookshelf. Not to mention, this book is filled with tons of stories and anecdotes that will make you laugh, cry, and contemplate.

Xenia Kozhevnikova,
Blogger, Journalist, Founder of the 'Xenia Did That' Project

ABOUT THE AUTHOR

Konstantin Kozhevnikov, PhD in Economics, is an economist, mentor, entrepreneur, investor, and author with a robust career spanning over 35 years. Konstantin has served in leadership positions across diverse sectors — including governmental, international, public, social, and private spheres—in Russia, the CIS countries, Europe, and Asia. He is renowned for his strategic management and adept problem-solving within various industries such as banking, real estate, investments, financial technologies, energy, resource conservation, and asset management, consistently leading complex, multi-industry projects to success.

Konstantin's journey began in the sporting world; he was a wrestler and later became the playing coach for the USSR national American football team. Alongside his wife Elena, he co-owned the 'Moscow Giants'. His initiatives weren't just limited to the field; he pioneered the first-ever television programs for American football in the USSR, playing a pivotal role in the sport's regional development. From 2003 to 2011, he chaired the Russian Golf Association. Under his leadership the Russian golf market burgeoned, reaching over one billion dollars in value. He was crucial in helping found new golf clubs in Russia and implementing a unified handicap accounting system, significantly boosting the sport's popularity across the CIS.

Married for nearly 40 years to Elena Kozhevnikova, an accomplished artist, photographer, designer, and digital content creator, Konstantin is a family man. Their daughter, Xenia, a women's rights advocate and pro wrestling journalist, continues the family tradition of breaking boundaries and creating impactful content. This blend of cultural, sporting, and artistic endeavors is a testament to Konstantin's multifaceted life and illustrious career.

CONTENTS

*To my parents and older sister who
raised me with the confidence that
anything is possible.*

*To my wife Elena and our daughter Xenia:
Your unconditional support, love, and faith
in me made this job possible.*

FROM THE AUTHOR

No one would argue with the fact that our life is incredibly diverse. There's no chance of getting bored with it. Life is filled with surprises — some pleasant, some not so lovely — joys and sorrows, hopes and disappointments.

Moments of incredible happiness can swiftly be replaced by mindless grief, and vice versa. Things that pleased us yesterday might become annoying today. We may tolerate a colleague's unpleasant habits for an extended period, only to suddenly erupt in indignation over one seemingly innocent joke. We might endure an unloved job or boss for years, only to abruptly declare, 'Enough!' There are thousands upon thousands of such situations in life.

This fantastic game, played by over seven billion people on the planet and offering us marvelous discoveries is life. Despite our life being nothing more than a moment from an evolutionary perspective, we still wish for our own moment to be as joyful, interesting, and harmonious as possible. I have not yet encountered people who desperately refuse to be happy, healthy, and wealthy.

What is happiness? It has been discussed, written about, and argued over since ancient times. Aristotle mentioned that happiness is the activity of the soul in the fullness of virtue. According to the 'notorious' Wikipedia, happiness is a state of 'the greatest inner satisfaction with the conditions of one's existence, completeness, and meaningfulness of life, the realization of one's vocation, and self-realization'. Everything seems simple and clear, but it's not. The phenomenon of happiness is studied by psychology, philosophy, physiology, sociology, religion, and economics. Hundreds of thousands of books, popular movies, and songs also contribute to the exploration of happiness.

However, considering this, how is it that almost half the people in the world are unhappy?

I firmly believe that every person is the smith of their own happiness. Continuing with the analogy of a forgery, we must sweat, burn, and endure bruises to make even the slightest progress toward the desired result. But does everyone comprehend this? And among those who do, how many are willing to make the effort? For those who've resolved to take control of their happiness, do they possess a clear plan for today, tomorrow, in a week, a month, or a year? Is there anyone or anything aiding them in this pursuit? I don't think so. How can my stories assist?

I believe that our life constitutes a constant process of evolutionary change, based not only on anyone personal experiences, but also on the experiences of others. For an intelligent and inquisitive person, anyone they encounter is a source of wisdom, and life is genuinely a challenging yet incredibly intriguing game. Moreover, every individual can and should attain happiness. I consider myself happy.

Like most of you, I wasn't born into a family of millionaires. I went through kindergarten and grade school, actively engaging in sports. In my twenties, I ventured to conquer a vast metropolis with a mere 15 dollars in my pocket, not by choice but having unexpectedly awakened in a different country than the one I was born in one day. I pursued studies across various schools, institutes, and academies, culminating in a PhD in economics. I've traversed multiple industries and companies, overseeing thousands of people. I have befriended outstanding athletes, musicians, artists, and 'ordinary' individuals. My wife and I have contributed to raising our daughter, learning from my mistakes and setbacks, seeking compromises, and devising solutions to numerous problems. I've encountered thousands of people, ranging from heads of state and prominent corporate figures to ordinary folks in small towns and villages. Overall, my journey has been one of learning and continuous exploration of life.

Nothing can be taught, but everything can be learned. Learning should be natural and interesting, akin to Victor Dragunsky's 'Dennis' Stories', written in 1959 and read by me in the mid-1970s. Besides daily sustenance, people will always be interested in the matters of security, stability, and self-confidence, as well as in themes of communication, love, cooperation, support, care, and affection. They will be keen on learning and exploring the world and society around them. They will find interest in travel, art, and beauty in general and be intrigued by personal growth, personality, and development themes.

I believe, no, I know for sure that all these aspects, along with freedom, equality, happiness, and success, can and should be learned.

Who is this book for?

I hope that my readers are primarily intelligent people. Have you noticed that we use this wonderful word less frequently nowadays? Beyond its primary meaning, 'intelligent', there are several other equally significant interpretations, such as knowledgeable, clever, understanding, and perceptive. If we were to describe our ideal partner, child, business partner, colleague, friend, or boss using just one word, we would employ 'intelligent' due to its beauty and brevity.

This book is for influential individuals who seek happiness and balance and aspire to become even more significant. Let me elaborate: I regard a person with an opinion on any social, political, economic, or life-related issue as influential. A more influential individual not only holds an opinion but expresses it. An even more influential person holds an opinion and expresses it convincingly.

The most influential among 'mere mortals' have an opinion, express it, are listened to, and, most importantly, are heard. Thus, everyone can determine where they stand on my 'scale of influence' today and where they aim to be in the future.

This book is also intended for entrepreneurs. In my framework, an entrepreneur is someone who endeavors to improve their life and takes responsibility for both their successes and failures. Therefore, a hired employee, an executive, or an official can also embody the essence of an entrepreneur in the best sense of the term. Not every owner, co-owner of a company, or manager of a large corporation necessarily embodies the essence of an entrepreneur. Entrepreneurs, in the broadest sense, contribute to improving the world around us, even if that world is confined to their family or close friends.

This book is for those who, while in the pursuit of uncovering and realizing their business and personal potential, encounter numerous questions daily. As Eugene Ionesco, a French playwright of Romanian origin and a distinguished figure of the twentieth-century theatrical avant-garde, noted, it is not the answer that leads to enlightenment but the question. I couldn't agree more.

I hope you find answers to some of these questions within the pages of this book.

THE THREE PARTS OF HAPPINESS

It's hard to find a person who does not desire happiness. However, strangely enough, half of the world's population cannot attain or feel happiness.

So, what defines this condition? Can we decisively and confidently determine whether a person is happy or unhappy at first sight? Or does it necessitate time, tests, or perhaps examinations? Do happy individuals consume or drink something special? Or do they possess some secret unknown to the other half of the world's inhabitants? Why do some achieve a state of satisfaction with their existence, finding completeness and meaning in life, joyously traversing the path of their vocation and self-realization, while others face repeated setbacks along this journey? Let us try to understand this in broad strokes.

A long time ago, when I was about five years old, I had a 'serious' conversation with an adult about communism. 'Lucky you!' said my interlocutor. 'When you grow up, you'll live under communism'. 'What's that like?' I asked. 'Well, it's when everyone does what they can, and everyone gets what they need', was the reply. When I got home, I recounted our conversation to my father, eager to hear his thoughts. I am trying to remember the specifics, but our discussion transitioned to the topic of happiness. With a chuckle, my father shared his formula for happiness: 'You have to have fewer demands, then you will have fewer needs', he said.

Over the years, I can count on my fingers the number of times my father has asked me for anything. However, one day, he called and inquired if I intended to gift him something for his 75th birthday. Upon my affirmative response, he expressed a desire to trade in the car I had given him a few years prior for a new one. I gently reminded him of his own 'formula'. After a laugh, he agreed, acknowledging that his needs had evolved with time. Consequently, my father acquired a new car, and I received immense joy and happiness from bringing him that delight. It also allowed me to reflect once more on needs and their connection to pleasure.

Many years ago, I was first introduced to the works of the renowned psychologist Abraham Maslow. Most individuals have probably encountered his hierarchy of needs, which, in his perspective, are inherent in each of us.

These needs can be categorized into three groups. The first is the so-called basic needs — our physiological necessities like food, water, sleep, etc., and security needs, encompassing a sense of safety, security, confidence, and stability.

The subsequent group is the need for connection, which manifests in social needs: support, care, and communication. This includes the need for respect, belonging to a family or group of individuals, and seeking love, affection, attachment, and cooperation.

And finally, a group of developmental needs, which we can fulfill through our aesthetic education and self-realisation.

It is worthwhile for those seeking happiness in this life to carefully examine the clues left by the great psychologist. Perhaps, through close and inquisitive scrutiny, these clues will unveil themselves as a prelude to a marvelous state of contentment, fullness, and meaningfulness. Are those the steps toward happiness that the happy half of humanity has already discovered?

'NAKED PHYSIOLOGY'

At the foundation of Maslow's pyramid lie our basic needs: physiology and security. Let's delve further into what our physiological needs entail and how they impact our level of happiness. Initially, we often think of food, water, and sleep. However, upon closer consideration, we realize it doesn't end there. The need to breathe, maintain a suitable body temperature, and shelter is also crucial. Moreover, bodily functions such as using the bathroom and the natural need for sex play roles in our contentment.

It's undeniable that specific physiological needs may vary in intensity based on factors like age, condition, mood, and other variables. This blend of needs, constantly shifting and intertwining each day or every second, influences our perception of happiness. After all, happiness, much like love, is a feeling we interpret as a state.

Our family folklore has an anecdote about 'naked physiology'. When I was 16, I fell deeply in love with my now wife. At that time, I was an aspiring young professional athlete aiming for success in the World, European, and Olympic championships. Consequently, my entire life revolved around these ambitions and objectives. Concerned about my plans, my mother initiated discussions with me regarding life priorities.

During one of these 'political information' sessions, seemingly having exhausted all her arguments, she exclaimed, 'How do you not understand? It's simply naked physiology!' I took offense at her comment. However, for over 40 years, my wife and I have always smiled at the memory, often playfully responding to inquiries about the secret of our marital longevity with 'Naked Physiology'.

Breathing isn't solely about the air itself; it encompasses the air's quality and sufficient exposure to sunlight. When it comes to food, it's more about what and how we eat rather than how much we consume. Our bodies primarily require nutrients, not just calories. Likewise, water quality and purity take precedence.

Healthy sleep is intricately connected to maintaining an optimal temperature. Even in less discussed matters like bowel movements, apart from regularity, comfortable conditions significantly contribute to happiness — sometimes just having access to a clean toilet. It's noteworthy that China, for instance, runs an extensive initiative to provide warm toilets to villagers, personally supervised by the Chairman of the People's Republic of China and frequently highlighted in the media alongside economic and technological achievements.

Try to take a fresh look and assess where you stand with these basic needs! What and how can be improved or adjusted in the realization of these fundamental needs?

After all, frequent visits to a cold or poorly maintained toilet, constantly interrupted by others, clearly hinder self-realisation and personal development.

WHAT'S ON THE PLATE?

I recently learned about International Pizza Day. Unfortunately, I was occupied with a golf tournament on that particular day, so we missed celebrating this holiday. Nonetheless, as the saying goes, if there's a will, there's a way, we could always celebrate it on another day.

Given that we don't indulge in pizza too much, the next day, just for the sake of the 'holiday' (ha-ha!), my wife and I visited our long-time favorite, yet not quite frequented, pizzeria. Upon ordering two different pizzas, we began leisurely enjoying the exceptionally delightful olives served at this restaurant. Apart from the indulgence, I had intended to snap some photos of the pizza. The pizza arrived rather swiftly, and it was only after consuming a few slices that I remembered my planned 'photo shoot'. Deciding that taking pictures of the partially eaten pizza was inappropriate, we continued our hearty feast.

Interestingly, upon hearing about the 'holiday' from me, our daughter who was in a different country, ordered pizza for herself that day. She, too, forgot to capture a picture of it and shared her 'confirmation' of the celebration without a couple of slices. Fortunately, forgetfulness didn't afflict us, nor did we endure starvation for several days. This incident sparked my idea to discuss the 'relationship' between modern humans and food.

Our health, well-being, mood, athletic or creative success, and active longevity are 90% dependent on what, how much, how, and when we eat and drink.

However, I've recently come to this realization.

Initially, as a professional athlete, I had intended to emphasize my seriousness about nutrition from an early age. Yet, I now realize that 30-40 years ago, most of us didn't even contemplate this aspect. Our eating habits were merely a blend inherited from the families, countries, and societies in which we grew up and lived.

A famous line of Ostap Bender, an opportunistic, yet lovable and street wise movie and novel character, 'Don't make a cult out of food', - most accurately reflects the situation in those days.

Now we live in vastly different times. We have dozens of favorite foods, drinks, recipes, cafes, restaurants, cities, and countries that evoke memories tied closely to gastronomy. Food manufacturers and retailers tirelessly compete for our attention and wallets, whether on TV, the Internet, in magazines, or in presentations, as if we could suddenly forget about food and cease visiting stores or restaurants.

Let's not forget! We've been hooked on this 'needle' since early childhood. Yes, indeed! Because food, particularly modern food, can be likened to a drug. But for the more sensitive, let's refer to it as a stimulant. Doesn't that sound more pleasant?

I will not detail my eating habits — what I consume, what I avoid, how much, when, and how I do it to maintain health, stay active, and remain in a good mood. My diet and routines significantly differ from what I perceived as the norm 10, 20, or 30 years ago.

Today, everyone should consider what they eat and why certain items should adorn their plate. Instead of mindlessly consuming everything the food industry offers, we should ponder our choices. We're all captives of our habits and preferences, and pausing and reflecting on these aspects is often challenging.

Occasionally, life itself compels us to contemplate, surprising us with illnesses. Ideally, it's preferable to focus on such moments and delve into understanding these concepts theoretically before harsh realities compel us to do so. Yet, convincing someone, of anything, especially in the initial stages of an addiction — be it alcohol or drugs — is arduous. It demands knowledge, patience, tact, empathy, and an exit strategy.

To embark on a path of change, one must first acquire knowledge about it. I often recommend several authors — Marva Ohanyan, Douglas Graham, Eric Edmeades — to almost all my family, friends, acquaintances, clients, and partners. Their works are valuable reads, listens, or watches.

IMPORTANT TO NOTE:

Marva Ohanyan is a biochemist and naturopathic doctor renowned for her authored books on natural medicine, including 'Golden Rules of Natural Medicine', 'Ecological Medicine: The Way of Future Civilization', and more.

Douglas Graham, an athlete, trainer, nutritionist, chiropractor, and healthy lifestyle advocate, has over thirty years of experience as a raw fruitarian. He created a nutrition system encapsulating the fundamentals of fruit-based eating, as detailed in 'The 80/10/10 Diet'.

Eric Edmeades, an anthropologist, speaker, and author, founded WildFit, a program focused on wellness and healthy weight maintenance. His book, 'To Sugar-Free in 7 Days', delves into these concepts.

SAFETY: THE FOUNDATION OF HAPPINESS

*There is a silence and a sanctuary within you where
you can take refuge and be yourself at any time.*

Herman Hesse

After addressing our physiological needs, it's time to discuss the second equally significant basic human need — security. I would liken these two sets of needs to the two legs of a person, both crucial for our journey toward a happy and fulfilling life.

Often, many things and phenomena in our lives or nature seem so ordinary that we overlook or don't ponder them.

From infancy, we unconsciously seek security, often finding solace in the soothing tones of our mother's lullaby. As we grow, our need for security naturally evolves with us. We rely on adults, relatives, or companions to create a secure environment.

Initially, it may seem simple and straightforward. However, as we mature, our needs also mature. We engage in physical education, or sports and form numerous relationships at school, university, or workplace. We begin dating, start families, care for our children's health, and acquire possessions like houses, cars, various household appliances, and utensils.

Those fortunate enough to earn more than they spend often worry about saving, accumulating, or increasing their earnings. Additionally, numerous other tasks, concerns, and troubles constitute a life we strive to make happy and fulfilling. A life where, at the end of each day, we can exclaim, 'Wow, that was great!' rather than sadly reflecting, 'Well, another day has passed, and life is slipping away'.

Recently, our daughter Xenia (Xenia Did That), a blogger, activist, and wrestling journalist, embarked on solo world travels. Initially, these were short, modest trips with friends. However, as her projects expanded, so did the need for transatlantic flights, layovers, and covering significant events involving tens or hundreds of thousands of people.

Indeed, modern communication tools enable us to stay connected, easing our worries to some extent. During one of our video calls, attempting to reassure us, Xenia mentioned, 'Don't worry, I always remember, the most important thing is safety'.

> **For our happiness, what matters is not merely physical safety but moral and emotional safety. Safety concerning health, family, work, property, finances, and other valuable resources.**

Alongside our physiological needs, safety stands as our second 'leg'. As we know, feet not only require warmth but also protection against minor wounds, cuts, or abrasions that, if neglected, can develop into severe issues hindering our journey toward happiness

ANYONE'S A FRIEND,
BUT NOT BEFORE A PECK OF SALT

*If you have a person whom you can tell your
dreams, you have no right to consider
yourself lonely...*

Faina Ranevskaya

Having addressed the basic physiological and safety needs at the foundation of our developmental pyramid, let's continue our ascent toward the summit. Fortunately, there's more.

The subsequent significant step on this journey is our need for social connections. Let's delve into this aspect. You've likely heard the typical saying that humans are social beings. However, have you ever contemplated what this indeed implies?

For most of us, picturing life without social interaction, whether online or offline, one-on-one or within a bustling group, seems challenging. We all yearn for trustworthy and dependable friends to be esteemed and respected at work and at home, where we can freely share our innermost thoughts or seek guidance without apprehension of judgment or mockery.

We aspire to achieve monumental feats or small victories — achievements that may be admired by millions or cherished by a single loved one. We all dream of loving and being loved, even if sometimes the object of our affection is a pet dog or a neighbor's cat.

We desire to take pride in our families and children and, certainly, wish to make them proud of us. We revel in boasting about the accomplishments of our workplace, the sports team we support, or the causes we advocate for.

These examples could continue endlessly. They vary, yet they share one crucial aspect: they are nearly impossible without people — spectators, fans, participants. Our social needs, our longing for connections, find realization with the aid and involvement of others.

In my youth, I attended several schools and institutes, driven by my athletic aspirations, which led me to relocate to different cities. Subsequently, I engaged in various roles and projects across hundreds of companies spanning diverse fields, countries, and cities, encountering thousands of individuals. These initial encounters and acquaintances varied widely: some were successful, others less so, some were fruitful, some not, some pleasant, some not, some inspiring, others awkward, some leading to unexpected continuations, others not. However, I am now unequivocally convinced that no encounter is ever useless.

Each meeting represents an additional step, an additional rung on the ladder of belonging. Furthermore, it is a necessary step towards fostering friendships, gaining respect, and experiencing love.

> **Paradoxically, despite the flourishing presence of social media, the prevailing epidemic of our times is the epidemic of loneliness. Despite our inherently social nature, initiating contact with new people remains challenging for many.**

Yet, challenging does not equate to impossible. Consider that your current friends and family were once strangers, and now, imagining life without them is inconceivable.

DO YOU RESPECT ME?

Moving on to the next crucial level: the need for respect. However, could we, as modern, educated, and cultured individuals, lack some understanding of respect? Let's explore.

When we hear the term 'respect', the first thing that typically comes to mind is a collection of norms or rituals that have been instilled in us since childhood. These rituals include saying hello, refraining from interruptions, obeying our elders, refraining from swearing (especially in public), aiding the elderly in crossing roads, and giving way to seniors and parents with children while commuting. Furthermore, the solemn question, 'Do you respect me?' becomes the peak of friendly conversations, especially in more mature gatherings. It all appears simple, clear, and straightforward.

However, each level of our developmental pyramid represents a significant step. The journey upward involves numerous small yet profoundly necessary steps, none of which can be disregarded by someone aspiring to master the art of respect. What are these steps?

It all begins with being the first to learn to respect others unconditionally and unreservedly.

Parents, grandparents, older and younger siblings, neighbors, and numerous others, known or unfamiliar, form part of our social circle, even if we don't hold much fondness for these individuals and occasionally find ourselves in conflicts with them.

I often advise my clients that initiating positive actions in various aspects of our lives is crucial. However, many people mistakenly believe everyone must earn respect before taking constructive action themselves. They ask, 'Why should I respect someone who doesn't respect me?'

But it begins with us! Take the initiative! Identify a trait, quality, habit, or behavior in your adversary, spouse, colleague, or disinterested teenager that merits respect.

Only through respecting others can we elevate ourselves to a higher level, prompting others to reciprocate that respect. This mutual respect often evolves into trust.

Respect, mutual respect, and trust catalyze achievements, propelling us forward more swiftly.

Ultimately, these principles guide us to the pinnacle of respect — self-respect. Don't confuse it with narcissism or egomania.

I wrestled when I was young and won my first tournament at 12. One of my teammates was also a champion in his category. The coach congratulated us on the Monday before practice, and everyone started applauding with joyful, boyish hoots. Seated on the mat, satisfied, I relished my moment of glory when I noticed my friend, who had also won, applauding along with everyone else instead of proudly accepting congratulations like me. In an instant, I felt surprised, embarrassed, and ashamed, and then I joined in clapping. It was one of the most valuable lessons I'd ever received, albeit unknowingly.

I'm grateful I had a few seconds to witness the essence of mutual respect, trust, achievement, and pride without words, admonishments, or reprimands. It was all present in the smiling face of my comrade, applauding appreciatively alongside his coach, training partners, doctor, masseur, team manager, janitor, and perhaps even me.

I firmly believe that respect, in its broadest sense, aids us in approaching the next pivotal stage of our happiness — self-realization.

ON THE ROAD TO SELF-REALIZATION

*When we strive to become better, everything
around us becomes better too*

Paulo Coelho

Having discussed the basic needs — physiological, safety, social, respect, and recognition — it's time to reflect on the following important group — developmental needs.

Imagine climbing Mount Everest; when most of the way is covered, it's time to rest at the base camp and prepare for the final stage — conquering the summit. Only some people reaching the camp conquer Everest. For some, weather conditions may be unfavorable; others may lack strength, experience, training, patience, or courage for that final leap. Some return the following year for another attempt, while some, unfortunately, perish, forever remaining in the icy mountains. Others may decide they've had enough of extreme sports, and so on.

Likewise, an individual's ascent to personal development and happiness follows a similar pattern. Not all of us will be able to reach our peak, becoming a mature and fulfilled individual. Abraham Maslow believed that the number of such individuals worldwide to not exceed one percent. But let's focus today on our own 'rest camp' — preparation for the climb to the summit of personal development and happiness.

> **This 'camp' represents our need for creativity and learning.**

These needs are more than an essential intermediate step in personal development. They represent a vast plateau where we can and should anchor ourselves without fearing sliding back down to the bottom of our 'mountain'. It's a platform from which we can look back at the path we've traversed, gaining strength, energy, knowledge, and understanding for subsequent attempts at ascent. After all, only some succeed at their first attempt, right?

Our needs for creativity and cognition encompass our need for contact and development. Essentially, this is our fundamental reservoir, akin to the 'guarantee points' in the popular game 'Who wants to be a millionaire'. Without the desire to learn, know, and explore, we would remain primitive creatures. How do we nurture these needs?

My first piece of advice: read.

Second, if reading isn't your thing, socialize and listen.

Third, consistently seek out new activities until something genuinely captivates you.

Develop your passions and yet again, devote your time to reading, drawing, playing soccer, checkers, or golf – whatever brings you joy!

Essentially, do whatever you want!

Become a professional amateur in something you love.

I was fortunate: I grew up in a family that cherished reading. My parents and older sister read to me until I was four when I learned to read myself. Books were my constant companions, with cherished favorites kept close, even read during mealtimes when my parents were absent. They accompanied me to training camps, on subway rides, and during journeys by train and plane.

Interestingly, I learned English during commutes on the subway and train while heading to my daily American football practice. Even when work constrained my reading time, I decided to buy books that intrigued me. It's become habitual to buy more books than I can read. They say the human brain can store up to 20 million books, so the potential for personal growth is boundless.

I often share the story of learning English on train rides with my young clients undergoing crises in their early twenties. Previously, we weren't even aware of such possibility. Today, intelligent, talented, educated individuals aged 20 to 25 are often ensnared by social and self-inflicted expectations. They grapple with depression while hastening to find answers about their fulfillment, purpose, and balance in their personal lives or careers. In older individuals, this might be termed a midlife crisis or a crisis of self-actualization at 50, but the commonality often transcends age.

It's similar to attempting to leap up Mount Everest in one colossal bound rather than witnessing, in the morning's rising sun, the radiant peaks of balance and self-realization after meticulous preparation. This involves overcoming the challenging ascent of basic needs and the need for social contact, establishing oneself in the 'camp' of creativity and cognition.

IS IVAN THE FOOL A SUITABLE ROLE MODEL FOR SELF-REALIZATION?

Do you know the phrase 'you can't jump above your head'? This is a fallacy. A man can do anything.

Nikola Tesla

Nearly 2,500 years ago, Aristotle, the ancient Greek philosopher, a student of Plato, and mentor of Alexander the Great, wrote that happiness can be attained by realizing one's potential. There's also a Caucasian toast: 'Let our needs coincide with our capabilities'. Could these centuries-old insights from different cultures guide us in pursuing a happy, fulfilling life and self-realization?

Let's look into this.

A crucial clarification is needed. I often ask my clients to name someone they believe is genuinely happy among their acquaintances. Surprisingly, many struggle to name even one person. I guide them through this exercise, and then we explore well-known historical or public figures.

This simple exercise uncovers a deeply rooted misconception, or, better to say, a myth. The prevailing belief among most people is that a fulfilled individual is a blend of a simple tone, telling jokes and anecdotes, and a clown from a famous fast-food chain.

However, a genuinely fulfilled person is not obligated to be in constant fits of laughter, living carefree like a village idiot.

A happy person is, first and foremost, an evolved individual who realizes their full potential on the verge of their capabilities. They constantly develop and expand their capabilities to more fully realize their potential across all spheres of life — fulfilling aspirations and needs.

We'll discuss the concept of a developed individual later. Right now, it's important to note that the harmonious development of all spheres — physiology, and safety, needs for contact and development, self-realization, and subsequent self-actualization — leads us to the FEELING of happiness.

Happiness is like love in the famous song: precisely what it seems. It resembles a childhood favorite birthday cake with candles; each slice represents one of the mentioned spheres. Every slice heightens the sweetness and intensifies the flavor, offering that delightful taste of absolute and more intense, if you will, happiness.

Rarely can anyone consume a whole cake at once, but I've never met a person who would be happy to be congratulated with half or a quarter of a cake, even though they know they can't eat the whole thing.

Many areas in our lives simply have to exist, yet they often become so habitual that we forget about them or stop giving them importance until life surprises us with an unpleasant event.

For instance, if your phone or computer is stolen, your needs for security and contact are jeopardized, significantly dropping your happiness level. Furthermore, suppose the laptop or phone serves as a means of production for you.

In that case, your self-realisation needs also suffer damage, and restoring the desired level of happiness will require time and effort.

Speaking of self-realisation, let's delve into a crucial element: aesthetics development. Surprisingly, this vital aspect is often underestimated or overlooked by many individuals on the path to self-development.

So, what exactly is this concept?

When considering our aesthetic needs, our initial thoughts often gravitate toward various arts: literature, music, and painting. However, the realm is far-reaching and comprehensive. It encompasses theater, cinema, physical education, sports, travel, museums, wildlife observation, hobbies such as cross-stitching, jigsaw puzzles, philately, modeling, and even studying obscure languages. In essence, it is anything that allows a person to cultivate their aesthetic sensibilities.

These 'receptors' enable us to read 'wrong' books, watch 'wrong' movies, and calmly discuss 'wrong' works of art, theories, and ideas that challenge the majority's beliefs.

ON SELF-CONFIDENCE

> *I was always looking outside myself for*
> *strength and confidence, but it comes from*
> *within. It is there all the time.*
>
> *Anna Freud*

During a conversation with an aspiring blogger about possible strategies, topics, and niches in the still-booming industry, we drifted out of the blue into the importance of self-confidence. This caught my interlocutor more off guard than myself, as I firmly believe that self-confidence is one of the most crucial qualities for a successful personal and professional life.

When I asked the blogger to vividly describe his daily routine in a future scenario where he would already have ten million subscribers, he couldn't provide a coherent answer. He had never pondered such a possibility, nor did he believe it could happen to him anytime soon.

This brought to mind a brief conversation I had with my golf coach during a round together nearly 30 years ago. Being a beginner, I lacked the patience to 'see' the ball; prematurely, I would raise my head, looking into the distance where I expected it to go. 'Without self-confidence', my coach remarked, 'you can't achieve significant success in golf'. 'Without self-confidence, you can't achieve significant success in life either', I responded. We shared a laugh.

Back then, at 29, I felt accomplished, thinking I had earned enough to take a well-deserved year-long vacation and spend quality time with my family.

Then, my one-year-old daughter would hear my voice on the phone more often already she saw me. I would leave for work while she was still asleep and return when she was already sleeping. When I started golfing, I still didn't see her in the mornings. Still, in the afternoons and evenings, we enjoyed the warm Spanish autumn, happily exploring every possible corner of the hospitable island.

That conversation with my coach unexpectedly bridged the gap between my life experience and golf, helping me visualize the ingredients needed to become a more confident golfer each year. Right off the bat, I am still on this fascinating path.

There is a perception that self-confidence is a quality given to us from birth, like the color of our eyes or the shape of our ears. I do not agree with that at all! Moreover, as a separate and distinct quality, self-confidence does not exist in principle.

> **Confidence results from skills and competencies developed through personal and professional growth.**

I am talking about the most important one — internal confidence, fundamentally different from external confidence.

Unfortunately, the modern society is used to external confidence, which depends on a person's previous achievements, the assessment of superiors, and so on. But then I learned about golf:

> **Confidence is not the result of good play; on the contrary, good play is the result of confidence.**

Isn't it harrowing? Inner conviction in one's abilities is the result of many years of systematic training, a positive image of one's future and results, clearing one's mind of mechanistic clichés and patterns, using a benevolent inner conversation with oneself, a positive attitude towards life and the work one is doing, and, most importantly, believing in oneself.

And it's not just, and not so much, about golf anymore.

> **By cultivating inner confidence, we can learn to deal with the many fears that sometimes prevent us from becoming the best version of ourselves. We learn to harness the energy of these fears for our own benefit, to become stronger than our fear.**
>
> **We realize it will always be with us, but we are already out of its power.**

This true self-confidence can — and will! — be the cornerstone of your personality, which you can always rely on in difficult moments and periods. It is a confidence that will grow with you and will not disappear with one or two setbacks.

> **Begin by consciously visualizing your desired future in great detail.**

If you find looking 10-20 years ahead tricky, start with one day, one significant event, or a crucial meeting. This warm-up, which takes only a few minutes in the morning — right after waking up — or, conversely, before going to bed, will help expand the horizon of your dreams over time.

Let me tell you, it takes work. A small trick aids me in such instances. Often, when I want to begin something challenging and new — be it a new technique to add to my skillset or a fresh business project — I 'cheat'.

I say to myself:

> **'Try to do it just once!' Then, 'Try doing it for three days, five, a week, ten days, fifteen, two weeks', and so forth.**

It's hard to believe, but you'll notice the results within a few days. You'll experience a pleasant feeling of greater inner freedom, irrespective of external approval or judgment.

Next week, we've arranged to meet with the aspiring blogger to discuss when he will reach ten million subscribers. I'm confident it will be interesting!

HOW TO DRAW A PIG

Even in the company of two people, I will certainly find something to learn from them. I will try to imitate their virtues, and I myself will learn from their shortcomings.

Confucius

I can't draw. Absolutely not. It's especially amusing for me because my grandfather on my mother's side was a painter, and one would think I would have inherited some genes from him. Although I'd like to believe those genes have expressed themselves in other creative aspects of my talent!

Whenever people seek advice on making money or wish to join my mentoring program, I ask, 'Tell me about the business model you want to implement!' The responses vary from 'I don't know' and 'I'm not a businessman' to 'Why should I do that?' or 'I just want to make good money'. Then, I share my story about the pig with them.

It is believed that in the realms of art, literature, and cinema, only 36 main themes reflect the storylines of our lives. The renowned Argentine writer and one of the pioneers of avant-garde Latin American poetry, Jorge Luis Borges, argued that there are only four such themes, considering the rest as 'variations on a theme'.

> **I believe that even in our 'money' world, a limited number of effective narrative structures known as business models exist.**

These models have endured for a long time, seamlessly integrating into our daily lives, often to the extent that we overlook them. Unfortunately, we neglect to study them, instead engaging in empty theoretical discussions. Consequently, the majority continue to partake in others' 'dramas' for years, eventually transforming these into comedies, blockbusters, and occasionally tragedies reminiscent of horror films.

I appreciate a saying attributed to my favorite philosopher, Pythagoras, who lived two and a half millennia ago:

> **'Life resembles the Olympic Games: a few people strain their muscles to carry off a prize; others bring trinkets to sell to the crowd for gain; and some there are, and not the worst, who seek no other profit than to look at the show and see how and why everything is done'**

Let me explain how this relates to a pig. During my second-grade year of preschool, we were assigned a drawing task: to illustrate a story from a favorite work of fiction. I chose Ivan Krylov's renowned fable, 'The Pig Under the Oak Tree'. Now, the essence of the fable eludes me, akin to an expensive fragrance gradually unfolding its scent.

In 1975, though my choice was straightforward — I believed I could draw an oak tree.

However, depicting the pig proved to be an arduous task. Countless attempts yielded pigs, each uglier than the last.

Frustrated, I sought assistance from my artist grandfather, confident that he wouldn't refuse his favorite grandson. Finding him engrossed in the newspaper, I presented my sketchbook, hoping for guidance on drawing a pig, a task I was beginning to despise.

He glanced at my sketchbook and said, 'I'll take care of it'. With that assurance, I left for other assignments, anticipating his call to demonstrate how to draw a pig.

Time slipped away; it was nearing school time. Reminding my grandfather of my request, he returned the album with a smile. Opening it, my heart sank. Standing beside my oak tree was a magnificent pig — an outstanding rendition that 'shouted': 'No second-grader, especially not you, Kostya, could draw such a perfect pig'.

Pressed for time and with my grandfather leaving for a stroll, I reluctantly carried our joint creation to school, feeling uneasy.

'Did your grandfather draw it?' asked Anna Ivanovna, my art teacher, recognizing my grandfather's distinct style.

'No', I lied, earnestly.

'Let's see', she chuckled. 'Take your sketchbook and sit at the back of the class. If you replicate the drawing by the end of the lesson, I'll give you an 'A'. Otherwise...' She gestured with a raised index finger, indicating a failing grade.

I returned home with an 'A', boldly requesting it to be recorded in my diary. In 45 minutes, I replicated my grandfather's professional artwork of a pig in my own unskilled manner.

Spending years perfecting his skills, as had happened centuries before him, he would continue to do so. But now, my pig was in my backpack. This pig embodied my grandfather's creative experiences and those who had gone before him, influencing his work, life, and destiny, whether their impact was clear or subtle.

Even a second-grader can copy a drawing by a professional artist with time and effort. Similarly, copying working business models and money plots in real life is achievable.

> **On this journey, each of us needs guides. These guides are not atop Everest or hidden in impenetrable forests; they surround us everywhere. Our elders, parents, exceptional scientists, discoverers, athletes, and writers are in their works, books, poems, movies, paintings, and achievements.**

They could even be your neighbors, acquaintances, or colleagues who comprehended working plots and models before you. Tested by time, crises, and diverse people across different countries.

Consider this, especially when contemplating reinventing the wheel — or a bicycle.

SEVEN SIGNS
THAT YOU'RE TALENTED

We have enough talent to excel in at least one thing. The challenge lies in uncovering it. Those who don't grasp how to do that, spend years oscillating aimlessly and only bury themselves deeper. That's why not everyone becomes the best; many simply bury themselves forever and leave nothing behind.

Haruki Murakami

On March 16, 1969, the program 'Hello, we are looking for talents!' aired on Soviet Central Television. Remarkably, it was the first program of this format, hosted by a young Alexander Maslyakov.

For numerous participants — individuals from various professions — the program served as a gateway to the All-Union Youth Television Finals, while for some, it launched entirely new creative lives. Older readers will recall groups such as Aelita, Zodchie, and Yalla, who harnessed their talents in novel ways thanks to the program.

On the one hand, we are familiar with and frequently use the expression 'burying your talent under a bushel', describing a talented yet indolent or unskilled person.

Conversely, we might hear: 'You're good at everything, but you lack talent!' While this description is customary in creative professions, in other matters, particularly in everyday life, we feel uneasy employing this word — perhaps due to humility or because, like many —

It simply loses its original meaning.

Five or six years ago, I had to find a local manager and staff for a project in China.

> **Conversations with Chinese search and recruitment agencies led me to a surprising discovery: the best ones weren't just seeking employees for their clients but scouting for talent.**

If you have ever searched or are currently looking for a job in the former Soviet Union, how often have you come across advertisements seeking 'talent'? Haven't seen any? I can't recall encountering them either.

Today, I firmly believe that every individual on earth possesses talent. If you're already skeptically shaking your head, let's explore how to recognize natural talent within ourselves and others —

> **A superpower highly sought after by numerous companies and organizations, willing to pay generously, irrespective of crises.**
>
> **A talented person perfectly aligns with the defined criteria for a specific position or job.**

Their skills, innate or acquired talents, abilities, experience, knowledge, and, most significantly, aspirations harmonize seamlessly with the job they are undertaking or about to launch.

Consequently, it swiftly becomes evident whether a job suits you and whether you are a good fit, leaving room for only two straightforward answers: yes or no. No room for 'maybe', 'perhaps', or 'you should try'.

SO, HOW DOES ONE UNCOVER THE TALENTED PERSON WITHIN ONESELF?

Everyone would concur that talent is an intrinsic part of a person. So, who exactly is a talented individual?

In my view, a talented person is someone who:

1. Knows precisely what they want or actively seek the answer to that question.

2. Regularly question their manager or employer, endeavoring daily to comprehend even the minutest details, acknowledging that no detail is insignificant for a professional.

3. Understands that achieving their own goals and objectives is a byproduct of fulfilling them.

4. Continuously presents potential solutions to various problems and challenges to their employer or supervisor, disrupting the peace and offering new opportunities for both parties'.

5. Knows other talented people in their business, department, or organization; Communicates with them and regularly organizes various business and friendly competitions. However, 'who can drink the most beer' doesn't count.

6. Recognizes that they are a talented person. They don't feel the need to shout it from the rooftops. It's already evident to everyone through their calm and confident speech, how they stand tall with their head held high.

7. Most importantly, apart from their personal development, they're ready — no, they're eager — to assist other people! Whether with advice, a story, a smile, or utilizing their skills.

Of course, not everyone will be fortunate enough to discover their job, profession, or occupation on the first attempt. It takes time — not just a day or a week. I think actively searching for your ideal job over three to four months is perfectly acceptable.

Often, the rush, misunderstanding, or disbelief in the existence of an ideal profession or employer leads many people to lower the standards of their dreams, goals, and aspirations.

> **Believe in yourself and your future, even if it takes one, two, ten, or perhaps a hundred unsuccessful attempts. Through these endeavors, we approach the most crucial — the 'scoring' attempt. And always remember, you are a talented person.**

TARGET AS PURPOSE AND TARGET AS AIM

Golf is undeniably one of the most captivating and thrilling games on earth. At times, I hesitate to refer to golf as merely a game — it represents a vast universe, akin to a realm encompassing countless discovered planets alongside tantalizing and enigmatic nebulae, galaxies, and stars. However, this realization often strikes me: our life is, in a way, a game itself. And suddenly, everything falls into perspective.

I aspire to explore some nearby 'planets' within this golf universe shortly. Nevertheless, the vast majority will remain mere specks in my golfing sky. Yet, this reality doesn't dampen my spirits. Instead, it motivates me each year, driving me to seek more effective methods and pathways to approach my goals.

My golf journey commenced abroad, and my initial exposure to golf, followed by subsequent immersion, predominantly occurred in English. Whether through terminology, books, instructional VCR tapes (how swiftly time passes!), magazines, or TV broadcasts, English became the language I processed and conversed with myself during practice or play. Rest assured, it's not a case of a split personality!

I allocate considerably less time to practicing on the driving range course than I used to. Instead, I endeavor to tackle technical, tactical, physical, or psychological challenges on the real course whenever the opportunity arises.

This approach helps me create situations that simulate 'combat' as closely as possible, situations that have occurred in the past and might arise in future tournaments and championships. Alongside my imagination, I carry two universal questions wherever I go — the European Championships or a simple club Stableford.

Intrigued?

The first question, always posed before any tournament, practice round, or Range session, seeks the broadest possible context:

What is your purpose?

This question holds utmost importance as golf comprises numerous distinct 'departments', each demanding specific and focused attention.

During competitions, my goals vary based on the tournament. They range from the simple and enjoyable objective of winning the tournament to practicing a new movement, stroke, or a fresh ritual for preparing specific strokes in a real environment. This includes developing new psychological or emotional behavior patterns, optimal tee heights for drives that suit the fade, and more. Typically, one round equals one goal, which often does not aim to win the tournament.

However, there are occasions when practicing a specific task during the first six or nine holes unexpectedly yields a commendable sporting outcome. In such instances, I often tell myself:

'Okay. Cease practice. Attempt to win this tournament'. This fundamentally alters the context. I shift my focus away from technique, statistics, or what I'd like to improve in my game. Instead, all my attention aligns with the new goal of winning.

And what's necessary to win nearly any tournament? To hit the fairway as frequently as possible with your first shot. Additionally, to hit the green first, second, or third on the par-3, par-4, and par-5 holes, respectively. These become my goals in the broader context. The club phase isn't crucial; what matters is a club that allows me to concentrate solely on answering the following question repeatedly:

What is your target?

In Russian, this question can also mean, 'What is your aim?' However, in this instance, the context is significantly narrowed to a specific point — the aim before each shot.

It might be the top of a tree three hundred yards down the left side of the fairway, the center of the green, a hill adjacent to the bunker, or any fixed target.

With each passing year, as I delve deeper into the concept of unity and diversity of goals and their optimal combination, this approach also works well in everyday life.

The simple question 'Why?' asked to oneself in almost any situation can aid in distinguishing the important from the unimportant, the necessary from the merely habitual, and the urgent from what can be delegated or postponed.

ON THE IMPORTANCE OF EMPTINESS

Thirty spokes share a central hub;
It is the hole that makes the wheel useful.
Mix water and clay into a vessel;
Its emptiness is what makes it useful.
Cut doors and windows for a room;
Their emptiness is what makes them useful.
Therefore consider: advantage comes from having things
And usefulness from having nothing.

Tao De Jing

In this age of digitalization, my love for paper books persists. A work of fiction offers me an almost tangible connection with its atmosphere. When flipping through a business book, I'm immersed in the typical working state of reading a document, where I can permanently mark interesting, important, or necessary points, thoughts, hypotheses, or statements.

Each new book is akin to the commencement of a journey into an unknown country, an exploration of a new continent or distant galaxy. It's an excursion filled with new knowledge and experiences and room for contemplation and reflection. Similar to a seasoned traveler, I embark on these journeys well-prepared.

As I pondered travel, thoughts of our daughter, Xenia, crossed my mind. Interestingly, the name 'Xenia' has ancient Greek origins. One interpretation suggests it might have derived from the Greek word 'xenia', signifying 'hospitable', while another theory links it to 'xenios', meaning 'wanderer' or 'stranger'.

Xenia, @xeniadidthat, embarked on her 'wanderings' at just a few months old. Children grow up rapidly. For her, new impressions, cities, countries, people of diverse ages, professions, and nationalities, souvenirs, toys, theaters, circuses, concerts, sporting events, cafes, restaurants, swimming, golf, soccer, table tennis, airports, airplanes, and numerous other experiences became her tutors — older or younger companions contributing to her growth and education. Over the years, my wife and I observed that each trip and journey became a significant leap in her development.

During our travels, we always found time to discuss our essential ideas, projects, and plans, along with engaging in conversations on contentious issues that arise in the lives of individuals, families, or organizations.

The shift in rhythm, a sense of relaxation, the anticipation of new experiences, emotions, and the sense of gregariousness create an atmosphere conducive to candid conversations. These discussions and reflections often touch upon the most challenging and sensitive topics — topics we may sometimes shy away from in our usual work routines.

Among these recent discussions, the memory of our six-hour flight from New York to San Francisco stands out, oddly enough, on an Alaska Airlines flight. Before the flight, as is customary, we perused the book, magazine, and snack store — a staple at almost any airport.

'You often ask me questions about feminism', Xenia remarked. 'If you wish to get the general idea quickly, you can buy and read this book', and she handed me a book by an African author.

The author, Chimamanda Adichie, is a Nigerian writer acclaimed for receiving awards from The New York Times, the National Book Critics Association, and numerous others. Her book, titled 'A Feminist Manifesto in 15 Recommendations', was a message directed to her daughter.

I read the book during the first two hours of the flight, and the subsequent four hours were spent discussing it.

Arriving in San Francisco, I stepped off the plane with my eyes opened to the sensitive topic of feminism. I felt immense joy and pride in witnessing our daughter evolving into a knowledgeable, opinionated individual, forming beliefs on numerous complex issues and gaining influence.

Now, returning to my 'book trips', my equipment for such endeavors is simple: a pen or a pencil. I enjoy making notes, underlining intriguing or controversial thoughts from the author, jotting down ideas that arise, marking references to future reads, and much more.

Emptiness plays a significant role for me. I prefer books with large margins and ample space between lines. Moreover, what truly excites me is the void at the end of chapters, sections, and parts, where I can freely delve into my thoughts.

> **My experience — be it in reading, business, family, or general life — has taught me that every individual requires a specific 'void'. It serves as a vessel to fill with their own 'drinks'.**

Over time, these 'drinks' blend into a unique cocktail flavored by knowledge, experiences, emotions, and feelings. This concoction never exhausts itself. There's an abundance to share with friends, family, or chance acquaintances.

HOW TO LEARN
TO SPEAK YOUR MIND THROUGH YOUR MOUTH

If you want to say a word to me,
try to use your mouth

Boris Grebenshchikov

Among the most cherished moments in every family's memory is when a child utters their first word — a genuine word, typically 'mommy', 'daddy', 'grandma', or 'grandpa'. Then came more complex words; for instance, our daughter's initial long word was 'dog'[1].

So, why do we all need the skill of speech? It's for exchanging thoughts, feelings, and information. Speech allows us to acquire and share knowledge, discuss humorous incidents, share stories with friends, tell jokes, or narrate ghost stories. It helps us negotiate, introduce ourselves or our companies, and even argue when things don't go as planned.

Nature, evolution, or the creator has given us this unique communication tool. However, possessing the ability to speak doesn't equate to knowing how to effectively communicate.

Over the years, I've observed that numerous conflicts arise due to the incapacity to communicate properly — with one's mouth.

It involves having the desire to not listen to the other party, but attempting to guess 'what they intended to mean' instead.

This applies to conflicts at various levels, from disputes among world

---

[1] - *In Russian, the author's mother tongue, 'dog' is a longer word - 'sobaka'*

leaders to arguments between business partners or children's squabbles in a sandbox.

Most of us have engaged in such dialogues at least once, where we listened to arguments, presented our own, and either agreed or debated fervently — all within our minds. However, these self-conversations can be more detrimental to relationships, businesses, or projects than we realize. As we persist in these mental dialogues, we unwittingly attribute different, often not the most favorable, qualities to the other person. This can escalate conflicts, fostering misunderstandings and occasionally evolving into outright hostility.

I learned one of my life's essential lessons on effective communication from the renowned satirist Mikhail Zhvanetsky nearly 37 years ago in Rostov-on-Don. However, Mikhail Mikhailovich had no clue about it.

It was a scorching summer day; the Palace of Sports, where the performance was held, was sweltering. The satirist, clad in a suit, appeared onstage with his legendary briefcase, pulling out a stack of sheets to read his works. Drenched in sweat from the spotlight's heat, he constantly wiped his forehead with a white handkerchief he never intended to pocket.

After about 15-20 minutes, he paused and, with his signature smile, said: 'Look, there are people here supposed to be cooling us down so we don't perish from the heat'.

The audience laughed, and he resumed. Unbelievably, a cool breeze wafted from the air conditioners a few minutes later.

He stopped again and said something that has stayed with me for life: 'That's how we always keep silent. But we should talk about what we want or what we don't like. Don't be silent'.

Let's face it: it's not easy. People tend to be shy, afraid, and doubtful of themselves, apprehensive of unexpected reactions or potential consequences. However, verbal communication can serve as a crucial tool for personal growth, aiding in enhancing self-esteem by practicing and building self-confidence. A self-assured individual stands on a higher ladder rung towards self-realization and happiness.

DO YOU WANT TO TALK ABOUT IT?

Have you ever wondered which words are most commonly used when congratulating relatives, friends, and acquaintances on holidays, anniversaries, achievements, and Christmases? I have long ago adopted the mantra of wishing them happiness, health, and love.

These three aspects are often considered the most important and necessary for a fulfilling life. However, it is worth considering whether there are other aspects that are equally important but overlooked. Alternatively, we may be too lazy to think of more complex desires. Perhaps our desire for simplicity leads us to focus on these three wishes. Every person on earth dreams of clear and simple things, such as happiness.

My definition of a happy person is someone who has fully realized their potential at the edge of their capabilities. This includes constantly developing and expanding their capabilities for even more complete realization of their potential in all areas of their lives.

'Happiness' is a complex concept. It is important to note that the concept of health, as defined by the World Health Organization in 1948, is not limited to the absence of disease or physical impairment, but rather encompasses complete physical, mental, and social well-being.

Additionally, it is worth noting that expressing love is beneficial for both happiness and health.

> **Now about love. How often do you verbally share your affection with your loved ones? When is the last time you've told them how much they mean to you?**
>
> **What are you willing to do for your family (and no, jumping off a cliff, doing extreme sports or drinking a whole bottle of vodka doesn't count).**

Some may argue that expressing emotions verbally to one's family is unnecessary, as they are already aware of their loved ones' feelings. People often claim to love unconditionally and for no reason, but I strongly disagree with this statement.

Why do we often fail to give our loved once the attention we should be giving them? Reasons may include the inconvenience and the uncomfortable feeling. Moreover, sometimes there is no time.

However, each of us would like to receive confirmation that we are loved on a regular basis, even if it is only verbal. The key word here is 'regular', not just once a year on a holiday.

Try to express your love to your loved ones at least once or twice a day for a month, telling them how happy you are to be near them, how lucky you feel, and how grateful you are to God, fate or the universe for this precious gift. Keep in mind that it is not just a gift — it is a blessing.

Discuss love, celebrate and cherish it.

ABOUT PHYSICS & PHYSICISTS

'To a smart man, everyone he meets is a sage'.

Proverb

From early childhood, we are subjected to simple physical experiments that often result in bruises and abrasions. As we mature, our understanding of the subject expands both theoretically and practically. Physics is everywhere, around us, in us and with us, whether we think about it or not. This is also applicable to sports, particularly golf. One of my strengths in golf is chipping and pitching, which refers to hitting short shots. Golf is an incredible game. I must admit that the complimentary remarks from my colleagues during practice or competition rounds are gratifying, although I am aware of the subjective nature of such evaluations. As my regular caddie and I often joke, golf can be a source of smugness. It is a fascinating game. I believe that having a mindset of sharing knowledge and tips with opponents is crucial. After a round, I am often asked for help and advice, and some of my comrades even come to play and practice with me. They have mentioned that they had never played with an amateur who'd had such a good short game. In such cases, I start by explaining a simple physics concept at a fifth or sixth-grade level, such as gravity. If you are not a golfer and were about to quit reading this chapter, stick around. This chapter is not about golf.

The brain can create unexpected associations. I recall one of my physics teachers from my school days, who comes to mind whenever I give my masterclass. This teacher joined our class in the middle of the school year, replacing our previous teacher who had either gone on maternity leave or to another school.

We all had our favourite and not-so-favourite teachers at school.

Opinions of classmates towards individuals were often divided, with some liking them and others not. However, in the case of this 30-something-year-old man, I now realize that there was a clear consensus of hatred towards him not only in our class but also in others.

> **To my surprise, after many years, I discovered that he was a true teacher, with a capital T, who not only taught physics but also aimed to teach us how to think, analyze, and take responsibility for our actions and deeds.**

Perhaps the formal nature of communication hindered our ability to appreciate the valuable insights in his brief monologues on logic, perseverance, accountability, information retrieval skills, and, most importantly, critical analysis.

However, as the adage goes, nothing can really be taught, but it can be learned. Few adolescents aged 13-15 realize this, and we surely didn't.

Now I like the saying 'To a smart man, everyone he meets is a sage'

> **If you are willing to learn, even a single piece of advice, thought, or word can significantly impact your destiny, life, work, and relationships.**

Despite my my personal 'processing' speed being somewhat fast, it took me a decade to appreciate the fascinating and informative nature of the physicist I once despised.

Professional golfers pay their coaches hundreds of thousands, and sometimes millions, of dollars over the years.

Why? Because these coaches help golfers hit one or two fewer shots per round. It may not seem like much, but over the course of a tournament, a season, or a career, this can make a significant difference in a player's life and the lives of their loved ones. It may not seem like much, but over the course of a tournament, a season, or a career, this can make a significant difference in a player's life and the lives of their loved ones.

In today's society, we often crave instant gratification, but it's important to remember that small improvements can have a big impact. I am content if I encounter at least one interesting idea at an event, meet one fascinating person in a month, or find one engaging golf partner in a year.

I firmly believe that there are no empty or random encounters, and that an unpleasant partner at a tournament is not a coincidence. Our defeats and mistakes often provide us with more than we initially realize.

THREE TIPS FROM THE SOVIET TIMES

> *When you've spent half your political life dealing with humdrum issues like the environment, it's exciting to have a real crisis on your hands.*
>
> *Margaret Thatcher*

I do not play golf on Sundays. On a personal note, I refrain from playing golf on Sundays due to safety concerns. I fear that if I continue to play golf on Sundays, I may return home one day to find my golf equipment stacked in a pile and a locked door! Plus a note: 'Go back where you came from' P.S. Ex-wife. However, that day was an exception.

On the day before the quarantine, when many public places in Spain were to be closed, I wanted to enjoy the great Mediterranean weather before a possible break. It was a special occasion, but unfortunately, it didn't work out as planned. They closed early.

During a pleasant 45-minute walk along the sea while waiting for the grocery store to open, as to make some use out of my unsuccessful outing, I reflected on the situation. It occurred to me, that was the sixth or seventh crisis we had experienced since the collapse of the USSR.

I wondered what lessons could be learned from past and present crises to better prepare for the future. My mind naturally structured the question by topics, including family, health, and safety, money, and business. All along with analysing information (not to be confused with rumours), assessing risks and threats, drawing up scenarios and thinking of contingency plans.

That's theory, but what about practice?

Each individual has their own unique life, priorities, character, habits, peculiarities, beliefs, convictions, stereotypes, and shortcomings. However, what tips can be universally beneficial for everyone?

> *1. Analyze the worst-case scenario, which is highly unlikely to happen. The important thing is that the truth is often somewhere in the middle, but you will be prepared for any eventuality.*

Ensure that you discuss these scenarios with your loved ones, making it clear that they are unlikely to occur.

> *2. In difficult times, it is important to remain calm. Therefore, the phrase 'Composure! Only composure!' of a famous character in a Soviet cartoon should be adopted as a motto. This ability is crucial not only for scouts, astronauts, pilots, and sailors, but for everyone.*

Scientific research has shown that experiencing emotions such as anger, nervousness or fear can significantly impair our cognitive abilities and affect how we make decisions.

> *3. Rely only on yourself and your loved ones, as it is not advisable to expect help from others. It is important to remember that there are always people who may require assistance more urgently than you do.*

There is greater satisfaction in receiving unexpected help than in expecting it as a given.

Always remember that a healthy level of struggle, used positively, can serve as an excellent psychological defense against all sorts of problems and disasters.

We will overcome this crisis.

ARE LOW EXPECTATIONS OUR WORST ENEMY?

*We were born to make
a fairytale reality.*

Pavel Herman

At one point in my career, I was involved in attracting investment for one of the brightest European projects. Despite my belief that the project was promising, we were unsuccessful in securing funding after almost two months of active work. I maintain an optimistic outlook and believe that every endeavour has its merits. One can either succeed or learn from the experience, making it impossible to truly lose.

While the market conditions were favorable in the past, I recall a conversation I had a year ago with a potential investor from the Forbes list, who is also an old friend of mine.

During the conversation, I presented the project to him. It is worth noting that my interlocutor spends a significant amount of time in the country where the project was based. Hel was familiar with about the location of our site, market conditions, prices, infrastructure, and other relevant factors. After he promised to consider the proposal, I requested that he consult with some of his affluent acquaintances regarding the project. A few days later, he contacted me and said: 'everyone's sitting on their money, but no one wants to invest, they're waiting for the crisis'. We shared a laugh and I expressed my gratitude for his time. We agreed to maintain communication and not lose touch.

And the crisis began shortly with news from China spread to dominate the global information, economic, and political spheres.

In the mid-1980s, Tina Turner released a song titled 'What You See Is

What You Get'. While in self-isolation at home, I pondered whether we truly perceive reality as it is. If we do this, we are more likely to exaggerate any event, perceiving every passing bird not only as a swan but also as a black swan.

> **Our subconscious mind enjoys stacking every news, fact or event into a pre-painted picture of what to expect.**

This phenomenon is known as the 'self-fulfilling prophecy' in psychology, first described by the American sociologist Robert Merton in 1948. It refers to a false perception of a situation that leads to new behaviour, which then turns the original false perception into reality. According to Prof. William Thomas, if people perceive a situation as real, it will have real consequences. However, self-fulfilling prophecies can also have positive outcomes.

Therefore, it is important to use this tool properly.

> **- Visualize an important situation and focus on the desired outcome, imagining that it has already occurred.**
>
> **- Mentally focus on the desired result by imagining that it has already happened to you.**
>
> **- Listen carefully and try to memorize your sensations.**
>
> **- Repeat the action multiple times.**

Like in any endeavor, nothing is possible without practice. But trust me it's worth it.

Because the ability to think about good things more often than bad (which is hard!) is the secret to the magic of the self-fulfilling prophecy.

I'll go and imagine something good now. So that it comes true.

BE PATIENT COSSACK...

Never lose patience – this is the last key
that opens the doors.

Antoine de Saint-Exupéry

Of course, we never thought that social distancing would last this long. For some time, our walks were limited to the supermarket. The road to the store passes by the golf club, sprawling on both sides of the usually bustling highway. At the point where the path slopes upward, memories of exhausting cross-country runs with the team in Tsakhkadzor come to mind, and I jokingly say to my wife, 'The incline is where you have to accelerate, endure, and overtake the others'.

I gaze at the emerald, glistening grass after yesterday's storm and think, 'Well, it's okay, hopefully, all of this will end soon. Focus on what you can do now. It's a great opportunity to work on your physical fitness'.

Throughout that time, every day, I chose one exercise and did it throughout the day. Over the years, I've learned to adjust the workout in such a way that the muscles ache slightly the next day, but it doesn't hinder me from playing golf or exercising other muscle groups. However, I won't give advice on what and how much you should do. The internet is filled with thousands of resources full of professional instructions to suit every taste. I'll say one thing: without patience and consistency in this, as in many other things, it's definitely not achievable.

Despite all the golf clubs being closed, I still managed to play golf every day. Please, don't rush to throw stones at me as a flagrant violator of quarantine.

| I do it in my head!

Every day, following the advice of my beloved Bob Rotella, a renowned sports psychologist, I select a golf course where I imagine playing an important tournament. These can be courses I'm familiar with or clubs where I've yet to play. The most challenging part for me in these mental games is the need to vividly and clearly envision the process of selecting the club, the practice swing, and the actual shot. For this exercise to yield results, it's crucial to also 'hear' the birds chirping, 'feel' the smell of freshly cut grass, and remember my sensations after executing a 'perfect' shot. Patience is key here once again.

Honestly, when I attempted this exercise many years ago for the first time, I gave up after the first two holes. Today, mentally 'playing' 18 holes takes roughly twenty minutes for a course I'm familiar with and about half an hour for an unfamiliar one.

So, as I passed the field on my way to the store, I mentally made a couple of birdies and reflected on how often in life, it's the lack of patience that hinders success. I'm guilty of this myself. And I've noticed that it particularly applies to talented individuals. Surely, each of us has had this dialogue with ourselves at least once in our lifetime: 'Ah, if only I had been a bit more patient back then, today…' And then, one can fill in the blanks as desired: I would be healthier and wealthier, a renowned athlete or musician, a famous actor, artist, or successful businessperson,

A vast number of people don't see things through to the end, abandoning their pursuits just a few steps away from the victorious finish line, which often lies just around the next corner.

THE KEY TO SUCCESS

Every person, even if they don't know of it or have never thought about it, has one or two most efficient ways of processing an issue or a question.

During the workday, I think best when I'm talking to someone about a topic that interests me, discussing a new project, task, or problem. Golf or a walk are also excellent exercises for reflection and visualizing the desired result.

In the early '90s, when I was taking my first steps in entrepreneurship, life brought me in contact with a person who had already had all the attributes of a successful businessman — classy cars, gold watches, expensive ties, a prestigious office in the city center, armed security, contracts with foreign partners, and much more.

Getting to know him better, I discovered that he had previously been responsible for the psychological training of the KGB forces of the most famous, as it's now commonly referred to, law enforcement structure. Always smiling, in good spirits, he radiated energy of absolute confidence, along with utmost precision and clarity in setting tasks.

I think he liked my wide-eyed enthusiasm, and the role of a mentor was customary for him. Once I went to see him to report on the progress of our joint project.

After hearing the brief account, my senior partner smiled and said,

'There's only one sphere in my life where the process matters and is interesting to me — the bedroom. In all other areas, it's the result that interests me'. Perhaps that conversation helped me focus on developing the ability to work for results, regardless of the industry, sector, field of activity, company size, or organization.

I also constantly analyze both the most successful periods of my work, prosperous deals and projects, and the not-so-successful ones, paying attention to common patterns and nuances. Two simple questions — 'what was done well?' and 'what did I learn?' — help increase effectiveness in subsequent projects and deals, enhancing productivity, bringing in more money while minimizing the expenditure of the most critical non-renewable resource — time.

I have a saying: when there's numbers, words are no longer necessary. Two parameters — time and money — can be quantified, setting aside engaging narratives and stories about the process of taking a bus, struggles with making calls, organizing meetings, and other 'heroic' actions on the path towards the ultimate goal: the result.

The ability to work towards results enables one to independently choose an employer, projects, partners, the field to apply one's efforts, becoming a truly motivated owner of their success and achievements.

HOW MANY CRISES OLD ARE YOU?

Over 30 years ago, when I was involved in American football, I was lucky enough to attend a practice session for a children's team in one of the hospitable cities in the USA during our overseas tour. At that time the whole world was admiring the ideas of perestroika and glasnost, and more likely, it was sigh of relief, hoping for the international tension that existed between the two superpowers of that time — the USSR and the USA - to ease.

We were welcomed guests everywhere, from the White House in Washington to a small gathering in a cozy little town, reminiscent of the 'Single-Storey America' from the beloved stories of Ilf and Petrov.

One of the exercises particularly struck me. The coach invited very young athletes, who were only wearing helmets with face masks from their specialized gear, to stand facing each other in pairs in the center of the field. One of the youngest players was asked to slightly crouch down and lightly headbutt his partner in the chest, more specifically with the face mask. Then, the boy who was hit was asked, 'Does it hurt?' 'Yes, it hurts!' came the reply. 'Get used to it! If you want to play football — get used to it! It will always be like this!' said the coach.

Later, becoming a coach, I always included this exercise in the initial training sessions with athletes who decided to try themselves in a new, rather tough sport. But the conversation now is not about football.

It seems to me that a similar exercise, even without physical contact, should be given to every child or teenager, telling them about the possible difficulties, hardships, and crises that practically every inhabitant of the Earth will face in life.

Each of us experiences from seven to eleven age-related crises in our life, sometimes referred to as milestones, during the transition from one age to another. Moreover, politics and economics can easily add a handful of various crises for each of us. Unfortunately, these periods sometimes extend over years.

But if you take a closer look at any crisis, it turns out that it carries not only negative but also positive moments. In fact, there are only two ways out of an impending crisis.

The first one involves analyzing the reasons, working on oneself, overcoming the crisis, and reaching a new level of physical, intellectual, emotional, and financial health and self-confidence.

The second, often used by people who, for various reasons, are not prepared for the fact that life is not the easiest thing, involves ignoring the reasons, suppressing their feelings, which can lead to unpleasant consequences.

Sometimes, a person who hasn't overcome a crisis begins, almost unnoticed by themselves, to lower their standards, abandon their principles, to deteriorate, seeking solace in alcohol or other stimulants. From there, it's a stone's throw away to neuroses and psychosomatic disorders.

Until the subject of 'life is tough' emerges in our schools, it seems to me that every parent should conduct such sessions with their children, a leader with their subordinates, a mentor or guide with their proteges, talking to them about difficult situations and crises they have OVERCOME in their lives, what they felt during those times and in those situations, what they learned, and how much stronger they became afterward.

WE'RE NOT AFRAID OF THE WIND, WE'RE NOT AFRAID OF THE RAIN

When I'm not on a business trip, I usually try to start my day with golf. This game is great because, depending on upcoming tournament plans, mood, physical condition, or company, you can choose and decide what golf means to you specifically on that day. It could be a serious competition almost at the Hamburg score, a meditative stroll, or a business meeting with a potential partner or existing client. An important factor here is the weather: wind and rain can spoil the mood for any golfer who isn't prepared for them.

Perhaps you won't believe it, but now I love precisely this kind of weather. But it didn't happen overnight. In 2011, I was preparing for my first European mid-amateur Seniors championship in Norway in early June. I checked the long-term weather forecast as usual and was shocked. Indifferent to my horror, the internet predicted 10-12 degrees with rain on all training and competition days. In the summer. In Europe. All in all, a nightmare!

But, as the saying goes, in for a penny, in for the rain. And I began to get used to it, especially since the weather in Moscow that year was also abundant with frequent rains, much to the dismay of many of my golfing buddies.

I like to joke that in the summer, I work like a pilot, depending on the actual weather conditions: good weather — golf, bad weather — work. Last year, everything happened the other way around. I remember how I was shooting hundreds of balls alone in the rain at the range at my local golf club. Then my longtime course caddy and I would go and play on the course, although the surface of the first Russian championship at that time was not known for good drainage.

Back then, I read a lot of available literature on how to play in the rain, starting from proper clothing, footwear, gloves, towels, headgear, protecting clubs from water, and applied it all in practice. Since then, I've had a particularly warm regard for Igor Chizhikov, who introduced me to the wonderful world of contact lenses, solving the problem of water flooding my glasses forever. Thank you, Igor.

All of this gave me confidence that we were ready to face the dire weather conditions at the tournament fully equipped. The most challenging task for me was the need to stand and endure the dripping or pouring water down my collar without rushing or forcing my strokes with all clubs, from driver to putter. Perhaps, after this preparation, I started to repeat more often that

> **In the modern rapidly changing world with constant 'winds' and 'rains', we must get used to feeling comfortable in an uncomfortable environment or situation.**

Therefore, now, if it rains or there's strong wind on the day of a tournament, I usually say to myself, 'Great! You are better prepared for this weather than others. Today, you have an excellent chance of winning the tournament'.

By the way, I often tell this story to executives and business owners who ask me about starting a business in China. However, I believe my advice about not letting external circumstances hinder your progress towards your goal can be applicable to a much broader spectrum of business and sometimes personal life.

HERE ARE MY TIPS:

- Seek professional advice from individuals who have had both positive and negative experiences in the market, field, or subject that interests you.

- Do your 'homework' and establish your level of stop-loss or boundaries in personal relationships.

- Practice under gentle conditions by rehearsing important negotiations or personal conversations, even in front of a mirror.

- Find your 'mentor'. It could be a local partner introduced to you by people who have experience working with them and whose opinions you value, or simply your friend ready to provide you with a second opinion, and so forth.

- If after completing the previous steps, the desire or intention to move forward remains, do so boldly and confidently. Remember, in self-development, there are no failures. You either win or learn something new that will be

HAPPY NEW YEAR!

Leading up to New Year's Eve, stores, streets, and social media feeds are filled with Christmas trees, lights, and decorations. Is there any wish, greeting card, or photo against the backdrop of a Christmas tree that you haven't seen in your feed ten times already this week?

Personally, I spent a long time choosing a photo for a New Year's greeting. My choice fell on 'Tulips' – a sculpture by Jeff Koons (by the way, my daughter's (@xeniadidthat) favorite sculptor), a bright representative of the movement that we broadly refer to as contemporary art.

As a husband to an artist (among other professions and merits of my wife @ekart.gallery), who creates precisely in this genre, I often encounter various opinions about it. I notice that people tend to, condescendingly chuckling, proudly declare, 'I don't understand this modern art of yours'.

For me, a situation where I don't understand something has always been a reason to read up, delve into the subject, and find information, rather than be proud of my ignorance.

But most often, this phrase leads me to another thought: does an artist, when pouring out their emotions in paint, metal, wood, or anything else, care about who will (or won't) understand?

I always approach my dreams and goals in a similar manner. My goals may be incomprehensible to someone, or seem unattainable or strange. However, the main thing for me is that I see meaning, logic, and coherence in them.

> **Just like contemporary art, your dreams or goals for someone else might appear as incomprehensible as a blotch on a canvas or a pile of scrap metal to some. The crucial thing is that you see them as a beautiful bouquet of tulips.**

WISHING GOOD QUESTIONS UPON YOU

I love questions. Everywhere and always, in all spheres and directions. I don't know what I like more — asking questions or when they are asked to me. I especially enjoy the right questions — ones that help reveal the breadth and depth of a subject, theme, reflection, or discussion.

> **A good question is like a perfectly executed pass, after which, as football commentators say, the forward only needs to put their head to it.**

As I wrote this, I remembered several wonderful years spent in my youth at a sports boarding school where aspiring athletes from all over the country studied and trained. At that time, I was involved in wrestling, and although our boarding school had representatives from all specialties, I mostly interacted with swimmers and footballers. One of the football coaches humorously used to shout at his players during the game, 'This isn't math, you actually need to think here!

It was especially amusing to remember his 'quote' during math tests when I habitually solved two variants, as the math teacher had cut off the attempts of my classmates to sit in a row across the whole class to solve the same variant as I did.

After the initial failed attempt and an uncomfortably large number of low grades, the process was restructured and 'technologized' by us. I had a special assistant whose task was to diligently copy and pass solved problems down the rows, without distracting me with the 'technical' work.

It's worth noting that this was done out of a love not for the subject but for sports because poor grades prevented us from going to training camps or competitions, which was the primary reason we were gathered at our boarding school.

Many years later, during very rare and often accidental encounters with my classmates, some of whom became world champions, European champions, and Olympic athletes, we recall these moments and share a laugh. Some might say that cheating is wrong. I agree.

But one of the main skills in life is the ability to determine and set priorities.

Our priorities then were training and athletic results. For me, studying was always easy, and I somewhat regret being too lazy to finish the last two grades of school with all top grades to graduate with honors.

I have always believed that the habit of reading, instilled from childhood, allows any young person to study well in high school, and not just there, without much effort. I am pleased that this belief and my story helped our daughter avoid the same mistake and graduate brilliantly from school with a gold medal.

Regarding questions, I will say that everyone who has worked with me knows that they can come to me with any question, and I am always ready to help and answer. With one small condition. It should not be the first question that comes to mind, but rather a question or questions that remain after some time spent contemplating and attempting to solve the problem independently.

> **Unfortunately, we often seek instant answers without putting in the effort, without challenging our minds, gradually becoming accustomed to intellectual**

I really like the statement attributed to Albert Einstein, saying that

> **If he had only sixty minutes to solve a problem, he would spend 55 minutes thinking about the problem and only five minutes solving it.**

Word of gold. Such an approach allows for the necessary 'breadth'. After all, as it is known, the greatest depth of a river is found in its widest part. Without breadth, there is no depth.

Very often, I hear the expression 'an uncomfortable question'. On the contrary, I believe there are no uncomfortable questions except for those you aren't able to answer. In all other situations,

> **A properly asked question at the right time can become your helper, a work colleague, psychologist, teacher, or mentor.**

Questions help us engage in contemplation, discussions on tasks, or issues. They provide necessary context to conversations or negotiations. They demonstrate your mastery of the subject or, conversely, emphasize a sincere desire to understand the situation.

In matters of the heart, questions help us learn more about a potential partner. In these delicate matters like love, interest and attention toward a person, the questions help break the ice, especially during initial encounters. After all, truly loving someone means getting to know them. Just as being loved means learning as much as possible about our childhood, dreams, fears, doubts, passions, views, and plans. And this can't happen without dozens and hundreds of questions.

The ability to ask questions requires a certain habit. It needs practice and a little effort. But did you think you could become your own best friend and be happy, healthy and wealthy without putting in any effort? Start with warm-up exercises.

> **Simple questions like 'why?', 'how?', and 'what for?' asked three to five times in any context, in any sequence, regarding any object or subject, problem, or situation will almost instantly help you understand your pressing issues more clearly.**

I am convinced that any questions, even rhetorical ones, are our assistants, invaluable guides to a better, more fulfilling, and happier life. Even if asked belatedly, like 'What on earth possessed me/you/us to get into this mess?' they assist in gaining invaluable, unusual, sometimes amusing, or even comical experiences. Experiences from which everyone can take something of their own, something they need, perhaps precisely at that moment.

After all, our life, like our path to happiness, is a continuous process of evolutionary changes, based not only on our experience but also on the experience of others.

LOVING EYES

> *You can only see things clearly with your heart. What is essential is invisible to the eye.*
>
> *Antoine de Saint-Exupéry*

Thirty years ago, my wife and I, still students at the time, went on one of our first joint vacations to the seaside. To Gelendzhik. It seems my mother found us a small rather cute, by Soviet standards, hostelry. The fact that the hostelry was a half hour drive from the shore didn't dampen our spirits at all. It didn't have its own beach, so we tried to diversify our days by finding new places to swim as best as we could.

Back then, we were studying in different cities, constantly busy, and the opportunity to spend ten days together was already a great gift for us. Nothing could spoil our mood, not even the less than ideal state of public transportation.

One day, while relaxing at the beach and flipping through a local newspaper, we found some amusing 'psychological' tests. Laughing, we discussed their results as they applied to us. Out of probably a dozen tests, I only remember one through the years. Each of us had to write down, on a piece of paper, all the best qualities of our spouse. By that time, we had known each other for six years, four of which we were married, and without much thought, I wrote down a dozen qualities that I admired in my clever and beautiful wife. We exchanged the notes and started reading them. What happened next was something I remember in the smallest details to this day.

My wife burst into tears. More precisely, she started crying uncontrollably. Bewildered, I tried to simultaneously comfort her and figure out what was happening.

When she, sobbing, could finally speak, she asked me only one question: 'Am I really as good as you described?' And then she cried again upon hearing the affirmative answer.

What does this story mean to me?

> **On the one hand, we don't often and clearly enough tell our loved ones what they are good at, what they excel in, how valuable they are to us, and how grateful we are to have them by our side.**
>
> **On the other hand, each of us needs a person — friends, spouses, parents, children, business or golf partners. It turns out that they can see something in us that we sometimes don't even suspect.**

For example, every three to five years, I conduct a 'sociological survey' among my friends and loved ones. I ask them to name just one quality or character trait that they think I possess. Our lives change very quickly, and any detail can help us avoid being hostages to our established habits. As it is known, our shortcomings are a continuation of our virtues.

Pessimists and skeptics may object that these assessments can be flattering and not always consistent with reality. Excellent! Perhaps that's exactly what each of us needs in the modern world, where streams of negativity overwhelm us from every angle.

> **Accept all the good things said about you as true. And cast doubt on all negative statements!**

On the eve of the holidays, try to resist the temptation to send the usual card or video via WhatsApp to your friends and loved ones. Instead, take a few minutes for each person, list three to five qualities that, in your opinion, they possess, and simply thank them for fate or the universe bringing them into your life. I'm sure neither you nor they will ever forget such a greeting!

GRANDMA'S PIEROGI
AND GRANDPA'S MILITARY JACKET

Amid trophies of war and the fires of peace
There lived bookish children, who never knew battles...

Vladimir Vysotsky

As a child, I loved visiting my grandparents. My love had four very serious reasons.

Grandma fried, specifically fried, not baked, delightful potato pierogi. Grandpa had a double-barreled gun that I was allowed to play with, a military jacket adorned with medals, and a tanker's helmet that I could wear anytime.

On one of the points of his Red Star medal, the enamel was chipped: apparently, a shell fragment hit it. Grandpa never talked about his wounds; he only explained to me what some patches on his jacket meant. At five years old, I didn't dwell on it, but the war, the wound, and the first medal happened to him at 26-27 years old! He was then half the age that I am now!

We often hear and repeat habitual phrases about how there's no present and future without the past, that nobody is forgotten and nothing is forgotten. But is it really so? How many of us remember our grandparents' birthdays? When did they get married? When did they meet? Where did they study and work? When and from where did they go to war? How and where did they fight? Where and how did they celebrate the end of the war? What did they do afterwards?

Honestly, all these questions truly sparked my interest for the first time at the turn of my 40s. Perhaps there was a sufficient amount of disposable income or maybe the infamous midlife crisis crept up. I asked my father to write down in a notebook and on a voice recorder the story of himself and my late mother, their parents, and basically everything that would come to his memory. Meanwhile, I started looking for professionals dealing with family histories and genealogy.

After several such meetings, I felt a strain. It seemed that if I were to say I was a descendant of Miklouho-Maclay or Przhevalsky's horse, I would be provided with all the necessary confirmations in a beautifully presented package within a tight timeframe. In short, it took me nearly ten years to find my historian. At once, I learned that my long-time friend, Andrei Stas, one of the pioneers of marketing in Russia, launched a company that deals with genealogy and archeography. Ever heard such a word? I hadn't.

So, almost 45 years after grandma's pierogi and grandpa's military jacket, I finally delved deeply into my family's history. My father had already passed away, and I haven't had the courage to peacefully approach his diaries yet. Afraid that someday we might simply forget about our distant and not-so-distant relatives, Andrei and I started working. Well, to be precise, researching, embarking on a journey into history.

In one of the photos of the brave Captain Ivan Andreevich Kozhevnikov from the Central Archive of the Ministry of Defense, I saw that same medal I used to play with as a child. In other documents, there was an autobiography written in his own hand, a record of awards and injuries. And plenty of other fairly formal information for that time, which after seven decades revealed new colors and emotions for us.

Some time later, we received more comprehensive materials from the still preliminary research. Surprise, delight, shock — these were just some of our emotions. My sister, who lives in another city, upon seeing them, called me and said, 'You've done such a great job! Thank you!'

By the way, one of my favorite movies as a child was 'Four Tank-Men and a Dog', the characters we portrayed while playing war games in our yard. And now, every May 9th, on Victory Day, I try to imagine my grandfather as a young man, bravely driving a tank like Yaneck. I mourn, I smile, I think about the past and our connection with the departed ancestors simultaneously.

Is it true that without the past, there is no future? Not entirely. There's always a future. The most critical question is, what kind of future? Why do we spend time and money searching for the past when there are already plenty of problems in the present?

Perhaps it's because the past is essentially our self-identification, without which the complete self-realization of any minded individual is impossible.

I often contemplate our family galaxy, our connection with our ancestors, with the past. After all, all our successes, achievements, and abilities are largely built upon the foundation laid by them dozens and hundreds of years ago.

The sun is not just one of the stars in our galaxy but the only star of the Solar System.

Other objects in the solar system orbit around the Sun: large planets with their moons, dwarf planets and their moons, asteroids, meteoroids, comets, and cosmic dust. Physics tells us that not only does the Sun influence the planets, asteroids, etc., but they, in turn, also influence the Sun.

Just like the Sun, we will always be connected by invisible threads to our family's past, the past of our country, our continent, humanity, our Solar System, galaxy, and the Universe.

It solely depends on us to turn these invisible threads into steel cables for us and our children, helping them move confidently towards inner freedom and self-realization. After all, these very same threads, if left unidentified, might turn into shackles on our feet, hindering our already challenging journey towards happiness. Helping ourselves on this path is very simple — **we need to know and remember.**

HOW TO MAKE THE WORLD A BETTER PLACE

Share your smile,
And it will come back to you more than once…

Song from the animated film 'Baby Raccoon'

Today, the experiment I've been conducting on myself for the last few months has successfully concluded. Not just successfully — stunningly so! Honestly, even as an optimist, I didn't expect such a brilliant result, and so quickly. Intrigued? Great!

Let me clarify that in the course of the experiment, no one was harmed, and everyone remained alive and healthy. So, here's the rundown! Almost every morning, I start with golf. I love being the first on the field early in the morning. I enjoy making putts on freshly mown greens and playing at my reasonably brisk pace. I don't have to wait if someone ahead of me is dawdling. A group of early birds like myself gathers, wanting to make the most of their day, to relish their favorite game before work and other chores and responsibilities. However, sometimes, due to time zone differences, I'm engaged in conversations with my Chinese partners or clients and miss the first morning tee-off.

Golf is a complex game, and it's nearly impossible to know all its regulations. Many of them relate to etiquette. But in my opinion, there aren't that many fundamental rules, and they are quite simple.

First: in golf, EVERYONE MUST greet everyone, regardless of whether you are acquainted or not. The only exception to this rule is if, for some reason, you simply didn't notice or see the person nearby. This can happen to anyone.

Second: you are obligated — emphasizing, OBLIGATED! — to invite faster players ahead of you. Whether you like it or not. Whether it pleases you or not.

These rules are simple and familiar to me, having become, as they say, a second nature. So I thought that in a rush, I simply didn't hear the response to my greeting from one of our club members. But seeing his grim face, I understood that he heard it but just couldn't cope with these simple rules. His face didn't just express dissatisfaction. It felt like he had lent me a large sum a long time ago, regularly reminding me of the debt, and here I was, not even considering repayment.

Honestly, I was surprised and even a bit annoyed with him, but I kept silent, moving ahead after an excellent (almost spiteful) swing with a three-wood on the narrow and challenging first hole. Calming down (and brisk walking really helps with that), I thought that maybe something had happened to him or he was just in a bad mood, so it wasn't worth paying attention to.

But in the next few days, the same thing happened again. That's when I decided to start my 'human study'. Thirty years ago, my wife and I, still students at the time, went on one of our first joint vacations to the seaside. To Gelendzhik. It seems my mother found us a rather cute, by Soviet standards, small pension. The fact that the pension was half an hour's drive from the sea didn't dampen our spirits at all. It didn't have its own beach, so we tried to diversify our days by finding new places to swim as best as we could.

A week later, along with the greeting, I wished him a pleasant day. Another week later, besides that, I started, again with a smile, asking how he was doing that day.

The effect was remarkable! He became friendlier, started smiling in response, at first a little tense, as if expecting a trick, and then relaxing and smiling fully. If we didn't meet at the start, we waved to each other from a distance, crossing paths during the round.

When I, satisfied, already considered the 'results of the experiment' satisfactory, my new friend completely amazed me. One day, seeing me at the supermarket, he approached me with a smile, extended his hand, and wished me a good day. For the first time, we shook hands. I wasn't just happy — I was ecstatic!

If anything in this story reminded you of situations with spouses or friends, at work or school, just remember that we are the creators of our own happiness, success, and mood. Just start first, and the world will surely change for the better.

STAIRCASE

I like the comparison of our lives to a staircase. Like an ordinary staircase with not very steep and fairly wide steps. With simple but reliable railings, like those in the panel houses that mushroomed in Soviet cities in the early 1960s.

An apartment in such a building became the first property for my parents, where I was brought from the maternity ward in 1967 (but that's a different story).

It so happened that in the cold season, we, as teenagers, spent quite a lot of time in one of the vestibules of our building. We talked, snacked on sunflower seeds, rode the railings, played various active and not so active games, mischievously rang the doorbells of neighbours, and then ran away, leaving a tardy friend to explain our innocent 'mischief' to the victim.

In the vestibule, we played tag and later combined it with another popular game called 'blind man's bluff'. The person blindfolded had to catch, tag, and then identify the caught player.

Another favorite spot for our gatherings in warm weather was the sports ground or any nearby vacant lot — garages, a boiler room, or a new construction site close by. It wasn't as comfortable and cozy as the entrance hall, but there was a sense of danger as we made our way through the stairwell among protruding fixtures and other obstacles. These risky games particularly attracted the growing, mostly male, generation of Soviet citizens.

We were fond of physical education and sports, so there were no drug addicts among us, and nobody called us that. Perhaps partly because in our area, there were several hostels for 'chemists' — a term used to refer to conditionally liberated or conditionally condemned individuals. They were forcibly employed in the abundance of industrial enterprises in the million-plus city. In general, both us and our grandmothers knew firsthand what drug addicts looked like.

But let's return to the analogy of the staircase and life. Bruises, bumps, strains, and sometimes even minor fractures were not obstacle for teenagers who knew every stairwell in our five-story building like the back of their hand.

In life, there are moments when you can jump over two, or even three steps. But when you grow up, it turns out that the measured ascent from one step to another is a much safer and more reliable occupation. You have time to look down, make sure that the next step is ahead, not an open gap that is very difficult, sometimes impossible, to overcome in a single leap.

The charm of the staircase of life is also that everyone can adjust the height, width, and depth of the 'steps' themselves. The speed of ascent, the rest time, or the preparation for the next step should also adequately correspond to the readiness of the 'hikes'.

AND HERE, IN MY OPINION, TWO ASPECTS ARE PARTICULARLY IMPORTANT

First: you must determine and always see your own Grand Summit that you intend to conquer.

Second: you need to move at your own pace, regardless of how quickly, or slowly, your friends, acquaintances, or neighbors are moving.

Remember, each of us has their own Grand Summit!

Therefore, the staircase that leads to it is also unique. Of course, you will need the skills and abilities to ascend your own summit. It won't be easy, but it's going to be worth it.

Study the experiences of those who overcame a similar staircase faster than you. Such individuals will undoubtedly be found. Their example can and should instill greater confidence in you. After all, if someone else could do it, then you can too!

The main thing is to remember that the most crucial step is ahead. There are no limits to this staircase!

Each conquered step is your new summit and a training ground for ascending to the next, brighter, and more appealing one.

GOT A LOT ON YOUR PLATE?

Politeness is intelligence.

Arthur Schopenhauer

Each of us every day gives or receives dozens of pieces of advice. Whether consciously or not. Friendly or not so much. Solicited or unsolicited. Helpful or harmful. From friends or co-workers. From spouses or from television screens. From the radio or the internet. Some people prefer to receive advice, while others prefer to give it. In general, advice is an integral part of our lives. Surely, each of us has the most favorite advice that we received in our life.

One of my favorites I heard from my parents in early childhood. Honestly, at that time, I didn't like it at all. But over the years, these words, like a good perfume, continued to reveal new meanings, facets, notes, and shades depending on my age, place of work, situation, sports I am passionate about, and other factors.

It's very simple.

| Worry about what you've got on your plate

This absolutely does not mean that you should NOT KNOW or SEE what is happening in other people's 'plates'. But today for me — I emphasize, today and for me — it means that it is I, and not someone else, who is responsible for filling my large family 'plate'.

For me, there is yet another meaning to this truth.

Recently, I won a small golf tournament organized with singles (meaning handicaps, not marital status) and professionals. It was a beautiful sunny day. Excellent company. The course, although long, was very familiar. The first hole — an incredible drive. Bogey. The third hole is a par-3 — bogey. Two over after three holes.

My flight partners — par and one under. 'Okay', I remind myself, 'golf is not about how you start. Golf is about how you finish'. Front nine — plus four. Back nine — par. Result — 76 strokes. I'm content. A great reason to remind myself: there were different meanings before. Perhaps new ones will emerge later. That's great. With this advice, I can also mentally return to my childhood at any moment when my parents were still alive. And I'm filled with a beautiful feeling of gratitude towards them.

> **In life, business, or relationships, initially, sometimes things unfold not as desired. But, as in golf, it's essential to keep playing, stroke by stroke. Worry about what you've got on your plate without tallying your own and especially others' scores after each hole. Enjoy the process. And only upon finishing, ask yourself, 'What did I learn today?'**

There were different meanings before. New ones may emerge later. That's great. With this advice, I can also mentally return to my childhood at any moment when my parents were still with us. And I'm filled with a beautiful feeling of gratitude towards them.

OH, THANK YOU, DEAR!

All our discontents about what we want appeared to spring from the want of thankfulness for what we have.

Daniel Defoe

Recently, I read that women say 'thank you' ten times more often than we men do. Surprised, I immediately conducted a small survey among the female members of my family. Both my wife and daughter were not surprised by this news, not only confirming it but also adding that ALL women notice this, unlike men.

Of course, the first 'logical' explanation that came to mind was that we men are simply ungrateful creatures. I thought I had never had a problem with this. But speaking seriously and contemplating expressing gratitude, I tried to remember all possible occasions when I should have said 'thank you' but, for some reason, didn't. Unexpectedly, I compiled quite a substantial list, starting from my parents many years ago and all the way to to the waiter at yesterday's restaurant. And while on the golf course, pondering this between shots, I suddenly thought about whom, among people from the past that I didn't personally know, I would want to thank if I could.

Quickly dismissing political figures of the past (too many 'blunders' with practically everyone), I turned to people in the arts. Writers and poets, composers and musicians, artists and sculptors seemed far more preferable from a distance.

Remembering that, suppose, I could only thank one person and bearing in mind one of the composers, I moved on to scientists.

Thinking about the hundreds of books by various scholars that I have purchased and, to my shame, still have not read, I recalled a recent conversation with my friend about Einstein. He discovered and described the complex, sometimes unfathomable phenomena or events that occurred millions of years ago. Suddenly, Nikola Tesla came to mind. Not just because I have a charger at home, in my garage in the storage room, that I bought in advance but changed my mind about purchasing the electric car, deciding to wait for a new model and a more extensive service network in Europe. How about that, Elon Musk, as they say.

Nikola Tesla is one of the greatest inventors whose works and inventions we use daily. The electric motor, radio, alternating current, and remote control — these are just some of his great inventions. Can anyone imagine our lives without all of this?

I pondered more in other categories. Names like Rosa Luxemburg, Martin Luther King Jr., and Nelson Mandela came up. As a golfer, I couldn't help but remember Ben Hogan and Arnold Palmer. But Tesla was still in the lead on my list. The final straw that tipped the scales in his favor was using a German high-frequency miraculous device to restore our cells' optimal balance.

It turned out that the waves discovered by Tesla are at the core of this device, which our whole family regularly uses.

They are capable not only of transmitting numerous informational frequencies, as in the case of a radio signal, but also wirelessly conducting electric energy, which helps our cells vibrate at the correct frequency, contributing to more efficient antioxidation and metabolism, improved cellular communication, increased energy levels, and much more. All in all, thank you, comrade Tesla!

All these reflections reminded me that perhaps the feeling of gratitude itself is a vital and, most importantly, beneficial emotion for our body. Lately, there have been numerous studies on this topic. Most scientists from different countries agree that the feeling of gratitude relieves tension, lowers blood pressure, and increases stress resilience. There are also scientists who believe that the positive effects of gratitude are slightly overrated. But even they do not deny that people who regularly experience a sense of gratitude are less anxious, more joyful, and satisfied with life.

But, without delving deep into the depths of physiology and psychology, let's just remember that a kind word is pleasant even to a cat. And for a social being like a human, especially so. But being grateful to someone for something good or pleasant is very easy. Thanking nature, the Creator, or the Universe for a sunny day, a rainbow, or a beautiful sunset is also uncomplicated. But gratitude for criticism, a remark, an error pointed out to us, for being fired from a beloved job, for a denial in something — that's a completely different matter. 'Thank you for everything', — such a phrase I heard a few years ago from an acquaintance. And the renowned Austrian psychologist, philosopher, and former prisoner of a Nazi concentration camp, author of the book 'Man's Search for Meaning', Viktor Frankl, even claimed that a person begins to understand why something happened in their life and what was ultimately for their betterment only after some time, after five or ten years. That's truly being thankful for everything.

Moreover, I believe that the feeling of gratitude specifically makes us more responsible for our decisions, actions, and deeds. This, in turn, brings us closer to the sense of fulfillment, contentment with the conditions of our existence, and a more complete realization of our life potential. Thank you, dear women, for that!

WHICH SHOT IS THE MOST IMPORTANT ONE?

To go back without finishing the task
was painfully frustrating.

Vladimir Arsenyev. Dersu Uzala

This morning, I made an eagle on a par-5. Any golfer knows how enjoyable that is, so why not brag about it? In 25 years of playing golf, this isn't my first eagle. Over these years, I've probably made dozens of them. They were all different but equally joyous. Today's eagle, however, gave me a reason to talk about golf and everything in due course.

The long par-five 13th hole on the course where I played today, with a good drive, provides a more or less decent golfer (which I consider myself to be) with an excellent opportunity to hit the green on the second shot, make two putts without much strain, and move forward with an easy birdie.

But my drive today was far from perfect. Landing on the far right edge of the fairway, the ball bounced sideways and, almost tauntingly, rolled half a meter deep into the only bush. Any thought of hitting the green in two shots was forgotten. Dropping the ball with a penalty, I instinctively glanced at the gadget on my left wrist, showing 211 meters to the nearest green edge. I encouragingly reminded myself that the crucial shot in golf is always the next one, trying not to get upset over missing the chance for a birdie.

I know the course quite well, so my blind three-wood shot to the left side of the green turned out decent, giving me hope to save par.

Having walked about 70 meters and spotted the green, I tensed slightly. There was no sight of the ball on or around the green. I almost thought it was a seagull's deed; they often mistake golf balls for other birds' eggs. However, as I got closer, I noticed the hole looked odd. It turned out my ball, hitting a slight slope on the left side of the green, unexpectedly rolled into the hole and stopped, bumping against the flagstick, slightly elevated above the edge. An eagle. Hooray!

Moving on to the next hole, I pondered that in life, we often throw in the towel after things don't go as planned, relationships don't work out, jobs don't go well, earnings or things we've designed for don't materialize. Or someone we're interested in doesn't show the desired attention towards us. Or a planned trip has to be canceled for some reason. And dozens and hundreds of various problems, hiccups, and failures.

> **And in these situations, it's crucial to remember that our most important shot is the NEXT one.**

After all, all the unsuccessful shots are already in the past. Yes, indeed! Otherwise, how would we know if they were unsuccessful or detrimental? We attached such a label to them. Remember, the next shot requires our attention, composure, and belief in ourselves. Even if nobody else but us believes it's possible.

> **One of the great golfers said that tournaments are won in the last three or four holes.**

Over the years, I've trained myself NOT TO KNOW my score until the end of the round. But the subconscious mind doesn't snooze. You still understand that the round is going well, and hope for maintaining a good result emerges. Knowing this, my wife usually asks me two questions after the tournament. 'Did you win?' she asks. 'And how did you play on the last holes?' And I have two pre-made answers to the second question.

If I played well on the final holes, I say, 'like a champ', if I played poorly, my response is, 'like a sausage'. These two concise definitions remain a humorous memory of my competitive youth. In golf, we often lose more than we win. Therefore, the ability to play the final holes well and reliably has long been a separate 'department' in my preparation, alongside driving, putting, and short game.

After all, you never know when it might come in handy.

In life, the ability or inability to bring a long-term project, deal, or promising partnership to a logical conclusion distinguishes winners from everyone else. In personal interactions, relationships built over the years sometimes crumble due to one silly word or action. Let's remember that.

By the way, I was a 'champ' on the final holes today. Made some birdies, finished with a par. 74 shots. Victory!

THREE CONSTITUENT PARTS

A man who works with his hands is a laborer; a man who works with his hands and his brain is a craftsman; but a man who works with his hands and his brain and his heart is an artist.

Louis Nizer

The first entry in my employment record book is dated April 1, 1986. I was a maintenance worker at the stadium. My mom arranged for me to water the lawn of the Rostov SKA stadium hosting the USSR Higher League football championship. Although that year turned out to be the last season for the army team in the Higher League, I was fortunate enough to see almost all the stars of Soviet football live: Lobanovsky, Beskov, Fedotov, Blokhin, Dasaev, Kipiani, Oganesyan, Andreev, and many others. But apart from this and pleasant 'strolls' on the perfect emerald lawn in the warm southern city, that job had another significant meaning — the opportunity to obtain, or as they said then, 'to score', a work record book with minimal loss of time and effort. It's funny to remember that now!

My watering colleague arrived at that job in a brand-new tuned-up 'LADA' car, with luxurious leather headrests, and did the job solely because of the employment record book. Both he and I earned our primary income elsewhere. During the day, my colleague was an excellent tiler, while my father and I glazed greenhouses, which still stand on the premises of one of the city's central strategic enterprises.

Then, I began to earn more than I could spend.

One of the reasons for this was an overall shortage of everything; there simply had to be something to spend.

But I admit that the possibility of earning a couple of thousand rubles a month stroked my ego. So, I even contemplated dropping out of the institute, thinking: 'Why do I need an institute if, after it, I'll be making 160 rubles a month?'

Despite having a physics and mathematics degree, my father led a brigade of, as they were called back then, 'shabashniki' (laborers for hire). The first thing that struck me on the enterprise's premises was the large number of workers doing nothing. 'Why do they invite us if they already have a lot of people on the payroll?' I asked my father. 'If the manager wants to complete a project quickly and efficiently, he hires us', — he replied. 'But they pay us ten times more than their own employees', I noted. 'Because they pay us for the result, and them — for showing up', he answered, smiling.

That conversation with my father, which happened at the right time, undoubtedly helped me understand a simple truth: many people are willing to pay tens of times more for the result than the process.

Since then, salary as such has ceased to interest me. I always aimed for my primary income to be tied to the results of my work. Almost 35 years have passed, and over more than a quarter of a century, I've managed people in hundreds of enterprises and organizations in dozens of industries and different countries. Fortunately, almost all of my employers were primarily interested in the result. They valued their time, and I tried not to waste it on endless negotiations about social packages and other 'privileges'.

Often in jest and seriously, I call myself a ' troubleshooting partner', considering my robust experience working with problematic assets, loans, and conflict situations, which, unfortunately, are once again coming to the forefront in these challenging times. I am not actively seeking work; it finds me. I'm not building my own corporation and don't need volumes for the sake of volumes. My motto is **'adding strategic**

value, experience, and expertise'.

Or, in the concise words of Luis Naiser, a lawyer, actor, artist, lecturer, and advisor to the most influential figures in the world of politics and business of his time, 'adding hands, head and heart'.

The format of my work can change depending on the client's or company's needs. The principles of working for results apply to the team, each member of which is a self-sufficient combat unit in their field. Partnership relationships and mindset allow me to be on the same page as business owners, asset holders, or real estate stakeholders. They appreciate that they can entrust something to me and my team, and forget about it, knowing that the job will be done. And if necessary, I will turn to them for help without staging a vanity fair or demonstrating my ego at the expense of results.

In the thirty-five years since that conversation with my father, it seems only one thing has changed: now I'm also a foreman. Or maybe even a master of my craft.

SYSTEMIC WISDOM?

*The tree must touch the sky and live with the winds
and the sun, without ever detaching its roots from
the Earth that gives it its place and existence: to be
the sky whilst still walking the Earth.*

Antonio Meneghetti

Periodically, I come across articles and discussions on the employment of employees and managers over 45 and the various aspects of this 'issue' from both the individuasl and employer organizations. This may be related to the pension reform, or maybe my 45+ brain, upon seeing relevant information, is trying to draw my attention to the matter.

At times, in jest and earnestness, I say that I've been leading people for more than forty years, recalling how, at the age of 10, I became the head of the squad council in a pioneer camp. It was a massive camp. While 'normal' kids were marching cheerfully to the beaches, I and dozens of my peers voluntarily sought ways to make the 'Pioneers' Journey through the Land of October' more captivating. We competed for the prized patches serving as a universal assessment of the squad's achievements, and my own.

It was a time now described as stagnation. Once, a mate from the senior squad approached me and proposed, as they might say now, a 'gray scheme' through which our squads would each receive the desired patch simply by reporting on a nonexistent joint project. Perhaps it was then that I first contemplated that maybe something was amiss in our 'conservatory', I don't recall precisely.

More than 40 years have passed in the blink of an eye. On the one hand, I have never had, and I don't have one still, a specific date or age by which I plan to stop working. On the other hand, I often, jokingly and seriously, say that I work to save up for retirement for myself and my family. Retirement that will allow us to live the life we enjoy. In this serious matter, I have never relied on, nor do I rely on the state.

Being a pensioner is more of a state of mind than dates in your passport, and leading people and organizations is more of an art than a science. Over the years, I've not only encountered 'pensioners' in their thirties but also worked with 'youngsters' who were in their fifties, sixties, and sometimes even seventies, whose experience and wisdom I've always been able to count on. But with each passing year, it seems to me more and more that something is amiss again in our 'conservatory' regarding the optimal use of youth and experience. Particularly when compared to our eastern neighbor — China, where I've spent much time in the past few years.

I'm often asked, 'Why did you go there?' 'To see what the future looks like today', I respond. Also, it's due to the atmosphere of optimism that amazed me, the feeling of a significant shared mission, and the confidence that even more significant achievements await their country. Over these years, I've been to hundreds of different organizations, from small to gigantic ones, some of which serve hundreds of millions of clients in the capital and smaller (by Chinese standards, of course) cities.

Indeed, the scope and scale of what is happening in China today are astounding, from the unimaginable pace of urbanization and poverty alleviation efforts to the technological giants and solutions addressing environmental pollution. As a leader and strategist, the systemic approach has always amazed me. Notably, the systemic approach towards people.

Systemic approach to talent or the human capital? - you may ask

> **I believe that only the approach to employees as individuals creates the conditions to transform them into genuine human capital — capital capable of achieving wonders.**

Even if that capital is of retirement age. You wouldn't believe it, but the Chinese retirees, men, and women, neatly and cleanly dressed, engaging in tai chi, playing go, or animatedly and peacefully discussing something in the park, have impressed me perhaps more than many of the wonders of modern China. Their demeanor, unhurriedness, and tranquility express the pride of people who have done their job well, passing it on commendably to the grateful next generation.

Furthermore, after working or living in China for quite some time, you start noticing that the country hosts many diverse social organizations at all levels. The Chinese have imbued the proverb about knowledge and strength with a unique meaning and content.

No relatively significant leader or expert reaching retirement age disappears into obscurity; they either continue to share their experience in a different format or commence something entirely new.

A new life emerges in the vast ocean of Chinese entrepreneurship, supported by the government and officials at all levels.

When we speak about managing organizations, we increasingly use words like 'efficiency' and 'technological advancement' rather than 'art' and 'wisdom'. Wisdom and life experience usually go hand in hand.

We wouldn't want to throw out the baby with the bathwater, even if it's over 45 years old.

A CHRISTMAS MIRACLE?

At first, you believe in Santa Claus. Then you don't believe in Santa Claus. And then you are Santa Claus yourself. How often do we laugh at this joke, that's even more ancient than this festive character. Have you ever had moments when, after some time, sometimes several years, you accidentally opened a book you had read before, heard a well-known story, or unexpectedly found yourself 'glued' to an old movie on TV? I'm sure you have. Has it ever surprised you to discover an entirely new meaning, idea, or undertone in them? I believe it has.

As it often happens in life, the true meaning of many things is not immediately revealed but requires some, sometimes prolonged, immersion in the problem, subject, or question. Similarly, our evaluative judgments can vary by age, experience, perspective, or mood. Like a proverbial moon, every question always has another side. Let's dissect all three parts of this joke. I want to believe, no, I am convinced that this story is more so about us than it is about Santa Claus.

The first part is the early childhood period when we consciously begin to believe in something, in our case, Santa Claus.

During this time, our lives are in the hands of the adults around us — parents, older brothers or sisters, guardians, teachers, and older kids in the neighborhood or at school. Almost every day, we encounter wonders and new discoveries, like the first visit to the zoo and the first solo trip to the store for bread where you can take a bite out of the crust while carrying it home. Or the first bicycle, you can finally maintain balance when the supporting wheels are removed. Or the first crush, when at four years old, you want to marry your older sister's classmate because she has a beautiful name, Nelly, and you like sitting on her lap.

> **The second part is the period of adolescence, sometimes agonizing, with all the quirks of puberty and increasing responsibility for your school grades, actions, or sports performances.**

It's a period when you're focused on yourself, trying to make sense of a whirlwind of emotions, events, and plans. Generally, there's no time for miracles.

> **The third and, in my opinion, the most fantastic period is when you become Santa Claus yourself. It begins with the ability, just by dressing up, to give a bit of wonder to everyone who sees you.**

If you're a bit luckier in life, you can gift much heftier 'miracles' to your loved ones and those who haven't been fortunate enough to encounter their own Santa Claus in life.

I'm particularly close to the image of a person who, having become Santa Claus, retains or rediscovers that excellent feeling from the first part of our story. A believer that everything happening around us is indeed a genuine miracle. Grown-up children, the discovery of new meanings and interests, the novel joy of a new book, movie, or a new dish at a favorite restaurant. A new painting by a contemporary artist, the desire to learn a new language or practice yoga, the successes of people you assist with your work or advice. Or even the rabbit that regularly waits for you at the most challenging hole on the golf course, as if reminding you: enjoy every moment, buddy.

However, humans are social creatures; sometimes, we see people around us whom I call tired. This fatigue is not dependent on age, gender, nationality, or country of residence. You will understand who I'm talking about. Typically, these are skeptics-cynics-professionals in everything related to perceiving their world exclusively in dark tones.

Sometimes, these people are called toxic. Of course, we all have bad days, moods, or feelings — that does not make us toxic individuals. These people though can, with a single word or action, shatter your faith in yourself, your project, your partner, or your chosen one, finally. Have you encountered such individuals? I'll add that, often without noticing, we regularly feed these people by arguing with them, trying to defend our views and uphold our opinions or projects.

Should each of us consider ourselves as Santa Claus in such situations? After all, Santa Claus is a true magician and wizard, bringing a bit of magic to everyone on an individual order.

What is magic? It is the belief in oneself.

We are born to turn a fairy tale into reality. But without faith in oneself and miracles, this is hardly possible.

COME, LET'S PLANT TREES!

The Love that moves the Sun and the other stars.

Dante Alighieri

There once lived a person who loved drawing, dancing, and singing more than anything else. Years passed, and our protagonist, the heroine, graduated from a music school, an art school, and a conservatory. With a vibrant appearance, a beautiful, powerful mezzo-soprano voice, and extraordinary diligence, a brilliant career as an opera singer seemed promising. However, fate, as it sometimes happens, had a different plan. Born in a country where socialism reigned supreme, one day she woke up and found herself in another, entirely new country.

The new homeland revealed thrilling daily opportunities for an enterprising individual, but classical art was not a priority for most citizens. Thus, nearly twenty years of daily hard work swiftly passed with little impact. Our heroine married her beloved, and together, they plunged into a new sphere with unexpected perspectives, travels, and opportunities.

Years passed, new challenges emerged, and along with them, a new life gracefully turned towards her family. A daughter was born, and new apartments, houses, and cars appeared. Private planes brought them to resorts with exquisite hotels and villas. But occasionally, she felt a sense of creative unfulfillment and a fear that she was not living her own life. She longed to relive those exhilarating, stirring moments of creative exploration, victories, and achievements again and again.

She pursued fashion design and then moved on to jewelry design. After twenty years of education, she couldn't imagine returning to studying. However, she enrolled and graduated with honors from a university, majoring in design and fashion. She took courses at a renowned British art and design college. Her field was creative, but ultimately, it became more of a business, slowly but surely triumphing over creativity, sometimes forcing her to stifle her own song in favor of efficiency and commercial interest. Yet, the most intriguing part for her was the moments of creative construction when ideas, thoughts, dreams, and fantasies took shape, sometimes unexpectedly, in metal, gold, or fabric.

One day, years later, in a conversation with her husband, she casually mentioned that perhaps she enjoyed drawing more than singing in her childhood and that maybe, someday in retirement, she would happily draw for herself. As Christmas approached, 'Santa Clause' unexpectedly brought her a sack filled with paints, canvases, pastes, brushes, palette knives, and other art supplies, the purpose of which he didn't understand but vaguely remembered seeing something similar in his artist grandfather's studio when he was a child. He practically bought everything he could find in the art supplies store.

Stunned by the unexpected gift, she spent several days looking at it all, afraid to touch anything. Three days later, she mounted a canvas on an easel and started to paint. She didn't understand what she was painting, how she was painting, how much time had passed, whether she had eaten, if it was day or night outside, or who had fed her beloved dog. It was a dialogue with the Universe. Her dialogue. With her Universe. Many years have passed since that day. Today, she is a well-known artist, exhibiting regularly in Europe and America.

Why am I telling you all this?

The Chinese say the best time to plant a tree was ten years ago. The second best time is now.

Sometimes, we all need someone to help, maybe even push us toward what we genuinely WANT to do. After all, we're sometimes unable to see the log and the speck in our own eyes.

We constantly doubt our abilities, talents, and skills, and we desperately need a friendly look from the outside to help us understand ourselves. Understanding and living without regret for the 'years in vain'. It doesn't mean that life will become easier. As they say, that isn't promised. But it will definitely be more enjoyable. Just remember, the best is always ahead.

As for me, many years ago, I fell head over heels for a female student from a major southern city that is still known as the gateway to the Caucasus. Then, I fell for an aspiring opera singer. After that, I fell for a model from Moscow (honestly, who doesn't like models?). Then things snowballed — a designer and owner of a fashionable clothing and jewelry brand. Then, an artist. And it seems I'm now 'stepping in the same river' again. My latest love is the founder of an international art gallery and an Instagram influencer. 'There he goes again', you might say.

I almost forgot, didn't I tell you that all these women are the same person? My wife, Elena Kozhevnikova (@ekart.gallery).

YOU CAN'T KNOCK US OFF OUR PATH, BECAUSE WE DON'T KNOW WHERE WE'RE GOING

It ain't the roads we take; it's what's inside of us that makes us turn out the way we do.

O. Henry

Indeed, for this reason, many of us are impossible to deter from our path precisely. But that's just a joke. You can laugh, smile, and leisurely shift to other thoughts, tasks, concerns, or conversations. But as they say, every joke has a kernel of truth in it.

Each of us has experienced uncertainty, doubt, and sometimes despair of not being able to answer questions like 'Where and why am I going? What do I want? Who do I want to be?' This occurs in our professional or personal lives, sports, and art.

'How much money do I want to make? How much time am I willing to spend at work? What am I willing to sacrifice for this position?'

Seemingly, there's work, success, and money but no happiness. All the letters are guessed, but the word can't be named.

As we know, unanswered questions have arisen and continue to appear for entire nations and civilizations. What can we say about ordinary mortals? How can one be, and what should one do in such situations? How can one rediscover that delightful happiness that many, unfortunately, haven't experienced in a long time?

According to statistics, a quarter to a third of the population in most countries feel unhappy.

> **Usually, my first tip is to mentally return to a moment when everything was clear to you, even if it's been ten or twenty years since then.**

This journey into the past will quickly scroll through the most critical, joyful, and not-so-joyful events in your life and set your personal value scale for future actions.

Now, pause and ask yourself:

> **How do I want to live?**

For convenience, you can categorize questions like family, work, education, health, etc. Try to reflect on the critical aspects for you in the next 10, 20, or 30 years. Don't be afraid. Time flies faster than we imagine! Dream, let your imagination flow, try to physically feel the ideal supposed picture of your future:

> **Add as much detail as possible.**

The eye color of your significant other, the scent in your cozy home, the pleasant upholstery in your car or airplane, even the moment of receiving the Nobel Prize, finally. Visualization has long been widely used and works great in sports, art, and cinema.

Now, calibrate your own value scale.

Try to formulate, detached from common stereotypes, what success means TO YOU, what wealth means TO YOU, what an ideal marriage and family mean TO YOU, what a perfect job means TO YOU, what an ideal vacation means TO YOU, and so on. One of my acquaintances pictured themselves as a billionaire receiving the Star of Hero of Russia medal. In general, don't hold back.

After this, think about the antagonists of your ideal job, family, hobbies, etc.

Voila! Your personal value scale is ready. Now, you can prioritize and assign ratings to various spheres, even on a scale from one to ten, and transfer them to any convenient visualization and contemplation platform, whether a computer or smartphone. Revisit this document whenever convenient to ensure you remember what you truly want in your everyday routine.

As a result of this work, you might have your own elevator pitch of happiness, which can be used in any situation. Within a minute, you can describe your life in all significant aspects in 10, 20, or 30 years, whether in an interview or elsewhere. Be happy!

THANK YOU, COMRADE CLAUSEWITZ!

As we know, strategy is a long-term plan that encompasses a period of time. It can be described as a way to achieve a goal. The strategy task is to use resources to reach the main goal effectively. It is essential when there are insufficient resources to accomplish the primary goal. Sounds familiar? This primarily applies to those who, like me, believe they have insufficient 'available resources' to achieve their main goals. To those who have their 'available resources' in order, congratulations!

This year marks the 240th anniversary of the birth of Carl Philipp Gottlieb von Clausewitz, a Prussian officer, military theorist, and historian who served in the Imperial Russian Army from 1812 to 1813. His magnum opus, 'On War', published by his widow a year after his death, revolutionized the theory and foundations of military science. During his lifetime, Clausewitz was one of the few who recognized strategy as a science and formulated its principles. Considering the theory of strategy to be extremely complex, he constantly revised and adjusted his works.

So, how can my 'colleague' (well, in a sense) who lived a few centuries ago help us in our, albeit peaceful, but still challenging times? Perhaps through his four principles.

I QUOTE, WITH REDUCTIONS:

> *'The first and most important principle in achieving goals <...> is to exert extreme effort by immediately mobilizing all available forces'.*
>
> *'The second principle is to concentrate the largest possible forces at the points where decisive blows are to be delivered'.*
>
> *'The third principle is not to waste time. Unless delaying the matter is expected to lead to particularly important results, operations should be conducted as quickly as possible'.*
>
> *'The fourth principle is to develop each of the successes achieved with the utmost energy'.*

HOW TO BUILD LONG-TERM PLANS

*Everything that happens, happens at the
only possible time it can happen, and it is
always at exactly the right time.*

The Book of Changes (I Ching)

Beginning to middle of December each year, I assess its outcomes and outline the following year in broad strokes. In the last month of the past decade, in December 2020, I realized that my usual positive questionnaire, 'What was good this year? What did you learn this year? What would you like to achieve next year?' wouldn't suffice.

Additional responsibility came from the fact that if this December was the last one of the decade, then, subsequently, the upcoming January would not only be the first month of 2021 but also the first month of a whole decade. Planning would have to extend to ten years. I needed to adjust my wish matrix, which helped me clearly address perennial but peacefully conflicting questions in the categories of 'Family', 'Work', 'Education', 'Hobbies', and 'Health' over one and ten years. What seemed like a relatively simple and routine task of composing an annual plan in light of the approaching decade became increasingly complex.

I should have started with a ten-year plan and then narrowed it down to one year, but that required more serious contemplation and effort.

The brain, that 'lazy creature', as Daniel Kahneman aptly put it, was keen on completing this challenging task as quickly as possible and indulging in well-deserved golf tournament watch party for one, in Full HD, accompanied by a vase of red Spanish grapes.

My thoughts drifted to China, where I had spent many months working diligently and with immense pleasure in the recent years. I had visited not only the familiar cities of Shanghai and Beijing but also many 'small' cities with populations in the millions and a history spanning millennia.

I recalled the numerous Chinese programs and plans designed for 10, 20, 30, 50, and even 100 years. Remarkably, these programs coexist without conflict and complement one another. For instance, the 'Made in China' program extends to 2045, transforming China into the world's leading industrial power. How do they manage to go beyond general phrases with such long-term planning? They've identified vital characteristics, prioritized directions, highlighted five significant projects, and identified ten sectors where work will be conducted over the next quarter-century. This promises to turn China into the world's largest economy and a driving force in global development.

How can one not recall the saying, 'You live and you learn'? I believe the Chinese have fully realized it, observing the rivalry between two superpowers — USA and USSR — and taking the best from both sides for decades. Patiently and persistently building their dream country, they consistently amaze the world with various innovations, which essentially are evolutionary improvements not only of their own experience but also of others.

Ayn Rand, our former compatriot who became a prominent American writer and author of four bestselling novels, once said:

'Unlike animals, humans cannot survive by aligning their actions solely with the present moment. Humans need to set goals; they must calculate their actions and plan their lives'.

These are words of gold! By the way, apart from being enormously popular in the United States, her novels are reissued in millions of copies annually, comparable to the Bible. Ayn Rand's global recognition is understandable: her nearly prophetic insights into various fields — politics and economics, social relations, and business — combined with her engaging artistic style in her works. It's worth noting that her most significant work, 'Atlas Shrugged', took her 12 years to write. Is such an achievement possible without strategic long-term planning?

I always ask my mentees to share their dreams. Sadly, many people, especially as they age, lose this marvelous gift — the ability to dream. I mean dreaming big, without doubts, reservations, or other inhibiting factors. After all, our dreams are the true foundation for creating our goals, which can and should then evolve into long-term plans.

> **Dreams and goals are the energy for the human battery. The more of them we have, the higher, is the charge level of our life batteries.**

It is precisely the big dreams and goals that give us the strength to bravely endure unexpected blows of fate, as well as various unpleasantnesses and difficulties that arise daily on our path to happiness, freedom, and balance.

So, shall we go dream and plan? Big time.

HOW TO TAKE CARE OF YOUR NE<u>SAT</u>CITIES

*Speaking without thinking is just like
shooting without aiming.*

Miguel de Cervantes

I was just about to say that golf is the most complex and challenging sport in the world, but I don't want to offend enthusiasts and professionals from other fields. I'll say that it's one of the most difficult ones. I have something to compare it to. In my youth, I professionally engaged in wrestling and later in American football, which, as you know, are not the easiest sports.

Considering this is a challenging game, the tireless multibillion-dollar industry constantly offers an abundance of things that may help make this game more approachable and easier. The key word here is 'may'. Right away, I'll say that only some things help, but not always.

Over the years, I've tried dozens, if not hundreds, of different training and in-game gadgets, tools, and devices. I've read thousands of pages of literature and watched thousands of hours of video content and broadcasts. The very simple principle I always share when people ask for my opinion on a new gadget, book, club, ball, or other gizmo (sometimes some things can't be called anything else): **if it helps, take it**.

Knowing from American movies and literature that everything you can and will be used against you, I comment only on what, I'd tried myself. At the same time, I always add whether I liked it or not.

I add what is GOOD or BAD according to MY TASTE, leaving the palm of responsibility to the interlocutor for subsequent decisions on usage. You must be careful in this competitive golf world where your opponent could start a fight because you talked to his BALL. Just kidding! Only about the world of golf being competitive. The rest is a true story.

I currently have five or six golf gadgets that help me improve my game. Although it can only be conditionally considered a gadget, one of the most successful purchases over the years has been the book 'Winning the Battle Within' by Glen Albaugh and Michael Bowker.

The book contains valuable content, but we will discuss THE SAT PROCESS and the Five Seconds today. This acronym stands for Strategy, Aim, and Trust. In our context, Trust can be translated as 'belief in oneself, one's technique, chosen sightline, strategy, club', and so on.

> **The authors claim that the cause of almost all foul shots is either problems related to a wrongly chosen strategy, poor aim, lack of trust, or a combination of two or three factors I aforementioned.**

This principle has changed my game, my mental state, and my mood during competitive rounds for the better, and it gave me the feeling confidence to continue climbing the ladder towards fulfilling my athletic dreams.

But even more importantly, I acquired an additional, almost magical tool for instant analysis of all my affairs, plans, desires, and aspirations in all other spheres and directions.

In addition to helping me make decisions about several stalled projects, companies, and white elephant relationships, the SAT Process also gave me an excellent tool for analyzing incoming ideas, proposals for collaboration, business ventures, or partnerships. Through this prism, I look not only at myself but also at my decisions.

> **Three seemingly simple questions: 'What is the strategy?', 'Where are we going?', 'Am I confident in the future/current partner, idea, business?' — Allow me to see the answers instantly.**

Indeed, the implementation of any new tool requires training and cognitive effort at the initial stage. But after some time, it becomes a part of you and works automatically, like driving a car or brushing your teeth. Precise questions, arranged in a logical chain, immediately create a visual answer, triggering a chain reaction of correct actions.

Knowing and understanding that the human brain is a fantastic supercomputer is important. Our only task as operators is to constantly input data into it and learn how to read what it outputs correctly.

Many people and companies who come to me for advice don't have a strategy. For many large organizations, strategies exist for show and are not used as fundamental tools in decision-making. Hence, there are problems with 'aiming'.

> **In other words, our lives sometimes compete between the present moment's taste and today's mood. Success at work or in business depends on how close you are to the decision-makers, whether it's shareholders, top management, or a line manager, rather**

| than your talent, initiative, and productivity.

The absence of personal or business strategy leads to the fact that every day, a person is forced to ask themselves the same unanswered question: where are we going? All of this leads to insecurity in the employer and the project, resulting in growing doubts about oneself, one's abilities, skills, and opportunities. As a result, there is an automatic decrease in personal effectiveness and productivity, a lack of initiative, and alarming statistics. Almost 85% – the overwhelming majority of us – do not want to go to work on Mondays. How can we break out of this vicious circle of negativity?

Try asking yourself these three simple questions. I can't imagine my life without them now.

PERPETUUM MOBILE

To strive, to seek, to find, and not to yield.

Alfred Lord Tennyson

I'm sure that most people from the older generation have read Alexander Kaverin's book 'Two Captains' and have probably watched one of the several films bearing the same name.

Time flies fast, and many of us may not remember the details of the plot, all the characters, and other nuances of this novel. But the key phrase from this work, which has become truly famous, is likely etched in the memory of several generations of readers and viewers.

I almost forgot that the motto 'To strive, to seek, to find, and not to yield' is the concluding line of the famous poem 'Ulysses' by Lord Tennyson, which is also engraved on the cross in memory of the ill-fated expedition of one of the first explorers of the South Pole, Robert Scott, on Observation Hill in Antarctica.

What do we, modern people, have in common with the famous novel's main character and Antarctica's conquerors?

If we set ideology aside,

> **it's a difficult and challenging journey in search of the two most important things for every person — happiness and love.**

Yes, In that particular order.

My female clients often argue with me, insisting that love should be placed in the first position. My objections boil down to the following: love is a gift, and not everyone in this life gets true, profound love from the Universe. Happiness, on the other hand, unlike love, can and should be built with our own hands.

It's not easy; it's hard work. It's not without reason that conventional wisdom tells us that everyone is the BLACKSMITH of their own happiness, not a representative of some easier profession. But if you have a dream that has turned into a goal and understand the structure and the necessary algorithm of actions, then forging your happiness step by step is within reach. And a person pursuing happiness is much more likely to find their love.

After all, big goals, such as happiness and love, give us a higher level of energy that we radiate, sharing it with those around us, automatically increasing our chances and our ability to accept the magical gift from the Universe — love, which, in turn, makes us even happier.

I heard a phrase that really struck me: people actually choose each other based on their goals. They also select each other based on the level of energy they emit.

Is this the eternal engine humanity has been striving to find for the centuries? What do you think?

ON FLEXIBILITY AND ADAPTATION

*There's nothing whereas we see neither justice
nor injustice which does not change its nature
with change in climate.*

Blaise Pascal

When talking about why I love golf, I often say that a round of golf is like a slice of life. Numerous joyful and not-so-joyful events, an unexpected bounce of the ball, sinking a 200-meter shot followed by missing a 30-centimeter putt you thought was already in your pocket – the full spectrum of emotions, from the exhilarating excitement before the very first swing of the day to the frustration of shots that were perfect yesterday but are completely off today. I'm sure anyone who has played a round of golf or even spent an hour on the driving range can add their emotions to this.

Last winter, we decided to spend it in warmer climates in Spain.

In my 25 years of playing golf, I've experienced extreme temperatures, from scorching 45-degree heat to near freezing. In Spain, I usually started my round at 8:30 when there was already enough sunlight, and by 11-12 o'clock, I was, so to speak, done. The six-degree fresh morning air, still crisp from the recent frost, would warm to nearly twenty degrees by noon.

And if in the morning my outfit was no different from the attire of an ordinary Moscow golfer closing out the season, bundled up in a warm jacket and hat, then by noon, it was an ensemble perfectly suitable for a Moscow summer.

If you suddenly thought that I was being haunted by the laurels of the famous writer Vitaly Bianki, I assure you the conversation is not entirely about nature. The conversation is about flexibility and adapting to ever changing external conditions.

According to the laws of physics that I am fond of, the ambient temperature directly affects the ball's behavior. Without delving into theory, I'll say this: the ball's flight length decreases as the temperature drops. Depending on the air temperature, the range of distances for shots with the same club can vary by tens of meters. For example, I used a 7-iron for a 120-meter shot on the first hole at 8:30 and then used the same club for a 145-meter shot on the fourteenth hole at 10:30, with no wind in both cases and almost identical shot quality.

So, somehow I won an excellent little tournament in Spain, avoiding the errors often made in such cases. What are these errors?

Underestimating all the factors, inflexibility, and an inability to adapt quickly.

Let's set aside the inadequate behavior and emotionally unstable mood that lead to other accumulating mistakes like a snowball.

Every golfer has a distance they've honed for each club over the years. For example, let's say it's 150 meters for a 7-iron. And often, without thinking, we grab that club for the customary 150-meter shot, only to be shocked when the ball decides to travel 20-30 meters less and ends up in the water, rough, or some other entirely unplanned for spot. After that, there's usually another not-so-great shot or even several. The golfer is frustrated because it seems like they made a great shot. This mood carries over to the next hole, and given that in our game, EVERY shot matters, a good result or victory often goes at the window until the next tournament.

DOESN'T THIS REMIND YOU OF OUR EVERYDAY BUSINESS AND PERSONAL LIFE?

When, regardless of the changing 'weather' conditions, we continue to perform the same actions that used to yield the desired results not long ago,

When, for various reasons, we cannot understand and accept that the same efforts will unfortunately yield worse results in the current conditions.

When we attempt to prove to ourselves, our subordinates, or those around us that everything is fine with us, we continue to make one managerial or behavioral mistake after another, becoming irritated and unwilling to consider the changing external conditions.

When our internal insecurity or, on the contrary, our inflated ego from prosperous times prevents us from seeking professional or friendly advice from the outside perspective.

When we are ashamed of our confusion, we get angry about it, and our irritation spills over onto our loved ones and subordinates, sometimes leading to a chain reaction of unwanted events and consequences for our business, relationships, or health.

Returning to the golf analogy, professionals are much less likely to find themselves in such situations, and not only because of experience. They always have a second opinion in the form of a caddy, whose main task is not just carrying clubs, as many might think. The best caddies understand their golfer's state of mind, enabling them to provide one or two correct pieces of advice during a round, sometimes offering a tiny tip that ultimately becomes the key to victory or a strong performance.

I've been fortunate to have had someone by my side for 36 years, someone who isn't into golf, who has never carried my bag on the golf course, but who seems to know me better than I know myself. That someone is my wife, whose love and wisdom have helped me solve problems, overcome anxieties, and resolve doubts. Sometimes, her patient observation, such as 'You're irritated right now, so you might not be in a position to make the right decision', brings me back to a productive state.

Unfortunately, not everyone has their own trusted 'caddy' these days. Don't be disheartened; just keep searching. In the meantime, don't hesitate to seek advice from friends, acquaintances, or professionals.

WHAT DRIVES US FORWARD

*In such circumstances, there can be only one stimulus
for acquiring knowledge (especially knowledge from the
perspective of classicism, knowledge that doesn't have
immediate and direct application) - curiosity.*

M.E. Saltykov-Shchedrin

I started school at the age of six, which wasn't the norm at the time. Our kindergarten, by the wonderful name 'little stork', was located next to the school, and in the first few days of September, a fellow kid showed me the first-grade teacher returning from her lessons. The main object of envy for the kindergarten children towards the school kids was the three-month summer vacation, so on the next day, once again through the fence, I approached the 'acquainted' teacher with a request to take me in to the first grade. Apparently, I was convincing. She took me to her home (none of the caregivers thought to object), gave me a sheet of paper, asked me to write down all the letters and numbers I knew, and draw something.

Thanks to my parents and older sister, by that time, I was already a confident reader. After listing almost the entire alphabet and, for some reason, drawing a pink pig standing upright, like a person on long hind legs, I was admitted to the first grade. I happily informed my parents about it when I got home.

They didn't believe me. So, on the same evening, I had to take everyone to the teacher for confirmation since, in 1973, having a landline telephone was still rare. So, I didn't have a traditional first school day on September 1st. I have no regrets! Since then, for several decades, I was almost always the youngest in the schools, among my peers, and teams where I studied and worked.

I was lucky: all my bosses, with whom I have ever worked, supported me, and in return, I always tried to be an indispensable assistant and collaborator. Of course, like everyone else, I sometimes made annoying mistakes and failed. But they were more than compensated for by successful projects and solving problems that, before I took on the responsibility, sometimes lingered for years.

Over more than a quarter of a century of leadership in various spheres, I have had the opportunity to communicate with many intelligent, talented, and hardworking people. They seemed to possess all the necessary qualities to move up the career ladder, except for one very important one – initiative.

I am convinced that this is one of the most important signs of a leader and manager at any level who wants to become a 'marshal', as they say. However, initiative must go hand in hand with responsibility. It's also important not to confuse initiative with overconfidence. Let me explain it using golf as an example. There's nothing sadder than seeing a not-so-effective swing executed at a speed that clearly exceeds an unprepared person's physical and coordinative capabilities. There are many amusing videos on the internet on that showcase just that.

As they say, power is nothing without control.

Rephrasing the wonderful advertising slogan of a well-known tire manufacturer,

> **'Initiative propels us forward, but it's responsibility that helps us achieve our goals'.**

Unfortunately, I often observe a lack of understanding of what should come first paralyze employees. What's the point of taking on additional responsibility in the form of work, tasks, topics, or projects if they're not getting paid for it or have yet to be given a new position they wonder?

And they aren't given a new position because they haven't yet demonstrated this new level of responsibility.

Life isn't arithmetic, and if you're capable of seeing beyond yourself, changing the order of the addends can sometimes result in a significant difference. A well-timed and correctly formulated question, even to yourself,

> **'What else can I do for my company, project, friends, or family?' automatically leads you to an entirely different personal peak, where unexpected perspectives open up.**

Here, the sources or even predecessors of initiative and responsibility are worth mentioning — CURIOSITY and KNOWLEDGEABILITY. After all, curiosity is inherent in all living beings, and humans are no exception.

But it's precisely the love, the attraction, the thirst for knowledge, or curiosity that distinguishes a rational human being from our smaller brethren. These qualities are inherent in each of us.

And sometimes, parents only need one thing, apart from their love for their child – not to hinder the little one from exploring the world around them. To patiently answer the dozens and hundreds of questions that constantly arise. To support the child in any undertakings and whims is sometimes incomprehensible to us, as in my case with school.

The German philosopher and one of the most renowned thinkers of irrationalism, Arthur Schopenhauer, who lived in the 18th and 19th centuries, once said that every child is a genius to some extent, and every genius is, to some extent, a child.

I try not to forget about this.

TO HASTE AND NOT MAKE WASTE

You can do it quickly but poorly,
or you can do it slowly but well.
After some time, everyone will forget
what was done quickly, but they will remember
what was done poorly. And vice versa.

— Sergei Korolev

We live in a rapidly accelerating world and try to keep up with it. As a result, we attempt to accomplish tasks in multiple places or do several things at once. It's challenging for us to finish reading a five-minute article online. We follow a chain of embedded links to other websites, and after the third one, we can't even remember what the original article was about.

It's convenient. The 'creators' of news have already curated the news for us; all we have to do is scroll through our feed. Manufacturers of clothing, electronics, food, and cars, as well as industries related to sports and beauty, are not far behind. The list goes on endlessly. All for our convenience, so we can accomplish as much as possible in a day, a month, or a year. Rushing in everything and everywhere.

> **The downside of this acceleration and the desire to be everywhere at one is increased stress and poorly executed work that must be redone multiple times.**

And in the case of the inability to redo such work,

The cycle repeats itself.

So, what can be done, and how can we escape this insidious trap of hastiness?

Firstly, learn to hurry correctly.

What does that mean? Often, when playing in amateur tournaments or with beginner golfers, I notice how their inability to 'hurry correctly' destroys the possibility of enjoying the game. A good golfer typically takes three to five shots on one hole, which takes 12 to 15 minutes to complete. During this time, the shots take only a couple of minutes. It's during these couple of minutes that haste is particularly contraindicated. As they say, 'Take your time'.

But everything else in the intervals between shots should be done quickly. This is where, like in life, most of us encounter problems.

The inability to determine when you can and
should hurry and when it's absolutely
unacceptable not only distances us from
doing work well but also, unnoticeably,
develops a habit of settling for mediocre
results.

It creates the image of a 'specialist' who needs to double-check or redo everything. The ability to distinguish between moments where it's possible to hurry and where it's necessary to concentrate can be the dividing line between mediocre and outstanding results in work and life.

Secondly, you need to learn how to determine the level of optimal workload. After all, no one in their right mind would think of lifting a 200-kilogram barbell without appropriate training or seriously suggest piloting a charter plane. Unfortunately, in today's world, there are quite a few such 'marshals' whom others often try to catch up with.

At the same time, I've always believed and still believe that 'we are born to make the fairy tale a reality'. I always support attempts to reach higher, but only by 10-20% above one's own height. Such exercises help with athletic, personal, and professional growth and make it gradual and stable while increasing self-confidence and protecting oneself against the 'decompression sickness', which can sometimes take on the form of an epidemic in specific fields. Adequate planning doesn't prevent me from dreaming, for example, of winning the European Golf Championship.

But I remember that any result is a byproduct of the process. And if the process is set up correctly, the chances of success increase proportionally. In other words, I need to consistently qualify for the European Amateur Championship. Then, I go through the cut or preliminary rounds having to pull myself up by the bootstraps but simply playing at my usual level. Only after my subconscious adapts to this and believes that 'yes, we can', can I start planning for more ambitious achievements.

This applies to every aspect of our lives. We should derive joy and satisfaction from becoming an improved version of ourselves as we progress. Keeping this in mind, we circle back to the importance of adequate workload. After all, everything has a price: our own health, spent time, shattered hopes, constant stress, personal dissatisfaction, and sometimes, unfortunately, unexpectedly cut our lives short in the prime of our strength.

So take your time and play YOUR game!

TO RELAX AND HAVE FUN

In addition to my regular golf sessions, I'm also a regular viewer of golf broadcasts. Let's talk about the European Tour tournament, the Oman Open, where the trophy went to the 21-year-old 'hot Finnish guy' Sami Valimaki. This broadcast allowed us to analyze several traditional mistakes from the 'wanted it to be better, but it turned out as usual' series.

If I were a sports commentator, I could eloquently describe the twists and turns of the game on the final holes of the regular tournament and the dramatic battle on three additional holes that determined the winner. But I'm not a sports commentator, and we're not here to discuss sports. We want to become true professionals in a completely different game, one in which each of us has been fortunate to participate since our birth — life. We aim to become our own best friend, and not be a hindrance to ourselves on the already challenging path to balance and self-confidence. I can already hear my wife's voice saying, 'Enough stalling! Get to the point!'

So, the most exciting moment of the tournament and Sami Valimaki's brilliant victory was not the thrilling final for me.

It was the very first day of the tournament, when we didn't see him or hear about him much. And we didn't hear about him because he was in... 101st place after the first day. 101st! As you probably guessed, it wasn't quite a winning rank, so the network didn't 'waste' the precious air time on them. How many of us would fight without losing heart after such a first day? What do you think?

But he won!

So, shall we give the guy the 'Determination' award? Should we cheer for him, sympathize with the losers, and then move on? Would that be that right? No, it's not! After all, we're here to talk and reflect on something else, along with my favorite question: what did this situation teach us?

In my view (disclaimer), our hero, like any athlete, came to win. Well, why else do people engage in professional sports? But on the very first day, things didn't go according to plan (as often happens).

> **Perhaps realizing he couldn't win the tournament, our future winner RELAXED, lowered his EXPECTATIONS and began playing his REGULAR game.**

If you thought I used too much capitalization, please reread the previous sentence.

So, what lesson can each of us take from this situation? How can it help us in our daily lives? In personal relationships, at work, or in business?

Where does this unpleasant stiffness, uncomfortable tension, dry mouth, and rapid heartbeat come from at the most inconvenient moments? What prevents us from playing our own game or being ourselves, sometimes forcing us to jump out of socks at the slightest challenge?

There are several reasons.

> **Firstly, having inflated expectations of the outcome of a meeting with someone we admire, a potential employer, investor, or boss. As well as our natural desire to appear more attractive.**

We want to do better than we can, seem smarter, more confident, more talented, and so on.

> **Secondly, we do not understand or believe that each of us has an ideal lover, a perfect employer, an ideal partner, and dozens and hundreds of outstanding people, activities, and pursuits that are right for us.**

What should you do?

> **Try to remain true to yourself.**

I know it's not easy, but being natural or relaxed (not to be confused with being sloppy or indifferent) always works better than being tense and uptight. Naturalness helps us think more clearly and bring out our best qualities, contributing to the fact that with each passing day, we can become a slightly improved version of ourselves.

And most importantly, don't stop believing in yourself.

Just like our Finnish friend, Sami Valimaki. Keep playing, growing, and seeking your ideal people. Don't despair if it hasn't happened yet after one or several unsuccessful attempts.

Just remember that each attempt is inherently a successful one.

Any attempt brings us closer to the sought-after ideal, which can change our lives for the better in an instant and forever.

THE CUP

Dreams don't work, if you don't work

Stephen Covey

Over the years, I have read and studied a vast array of methodologies and research aimed at helping people find answers to pressing questions about health, safety, success, self-realization, love, and happiness. These questions even led me to various schools, institutes, and academies.

The knowledge and experience I've gained will benefit many people seeking answers to their pressing questions and concerns.

Typically, my conversation with each new client in my mentoring program begins with 25 questions divided into categories:

Physiology, safety, respect, belonging, and self-realization.

The answers obtained provide a clearer understanding of their personality and a situational snapshot. Afterward, we discuss the main areas, pain points, and directions for the upcoming work.

Once, one of my clients asked me, 'Can I ask just one question to understand who the person in front of me is?' I replied: 'I would ask about the cup'. He asked, 'Cup?' — He enquired, astounded.

When it comes to a cup, our brain automatically and effortlessly creates a specific mental image. We 'see' the cup, its size, the transparency or cloudiness of the glass, as well as the amount of liquid inside. With a bit of imagination, we can 'examine' the body of the drink. We can even imagine the taste and our sensations it evokes.

Take a look at any aspect of your life or a topic that concerns you as an imaginary cup. By the way, you can and should have multiple such 'cups'.

The quantity and quality of the liquid in the glass represent your current situation. Now, imagine a full cup – this is your desired outcome. What kind of liquid is in it? There can be different options.

Take some time to reflect, conduct a brainstorming session, and formulate your dreams in the afore mentioned area. Generate ideas, thoughts, options, and ways to 'produce' or 'acquire' the desired beverage.

Now, the most crucial step. Write them down on paper. Create an action plan, a list of specific activities, and practical steps to fill your 'cup'.

Do not doubt, criticize, or evaluate your ideas with statements like, 'Well, I can't do that', or 'No, that's impossible'. Believe that anything is possible! Just record all the thoughts and ideas that come to mind.

Sometimes, we try to appear more substantial by expressing our 'weighty' opinion on various issues, turning us into self-proclaimed fortune tellers of our destiny. These visionaries constantly doubt their strength, abilities, and perseverance and don't allow themselves to dream big.

Try to become a child again who wasn't afraid to dream. But remember the most important thing! In the words of the world-renowned author of bestsellers on practical life and business management, Stephen Covey, 'Dreams don't work unless you do'.

TO FAIL OR TO HESITATE?

Every part of life has meaning. It's important to be able to extract the meaning. If you approach what's around you with interest and love, everything will come together in structure. You may not yet know what it will be... But you need to understand that it's a complete structure.

Sergei Bodrov Jr.

The best way to prepare for tournaments is competitive golf. Once, we organized a friendly match between professionals and single-digit handicap amateurs.

I found myself on a flight with Sebastian Garcia, the winner of the first-ever away Russian golf tournament, the Russia Winter Cup, back in 2004. By the way, Sebastian Garcia was, for a long time, the only golfer in the world to complete a professional tournament round in 58 strokes. Golf enthusiasts may also remember him for his appearances in the Russian Open.

Another partner in our flight was Sebastian Ruiz, my first coach, with whom I made my first swing in 1996, and I continue to collaborate with him to this day. Many Russian and Kazakh golfers surely remember him for his valuable advice during the World Corporate Golf Challenge tournaments in Moscow.

The most challenging aspect for me in such tournaments is

Playing my own game without trying to impress more experienced or senior professionals, especially on the first few holes.

I handled this task well by making a birdie on the first, par on the second and third, and getting a feel for the putt on the birdie. Midway through the round, an unexpected hiccup occurred on a narrow, challenging par-4 hole. Although I made an excellent drive and a good wedge shot onto the 'blind' green, I ended up with the ball in the hole after a two-meter backspin. That was satisfying!

However, I failed to secure a solid finish to the round, shooting the ball out of bounds with a seemingly straightforward seven-iron shot on a par-3 hole, which reminded me for the thousandth time that there are no easy shots in this game.

Even when the final result is far from the best in my sports career, my usual round analysis always consists of two questions:

> **'What was done well today?'**
>
> **'What did I learn today?'**

Such an approach, as opposed to self-blame or searching for culprits for mistakes, helps us develop and become more confident from round to round.

One of the greatest golfers of our time, Jack Nicklaus, once said that

A golfer should have a short memory for mistakes and failures and an excellent memory for victories and successes.

So, what can we take from my favorite game, which I have been passionate about for over a quarter of a century, into our everyday life?

> **First and foremost, an understanding that any complex endeavor requires patience and time.**

We often want instant success, results, or victories everywhere and in everything. A superficial look at other people's successes and achievements, especially in the age of social media, can sometimes create the impression that someone became rich, successful, or famous overnight. However, upon closer examination, it almost always turns out that this 'instant' success took someone 10 or 20 not-so-easy years to achieve.

> **Secondly, constant and close observation of oneself. Studying one's strengths and weaknesses.**

And here, we also need the help of friends, acquaintances, or colleagues at work. After all, each of us has four parts, as described in the so-called 'Johari Window' created by psychologists Joseph Luft and Harrington Ingham in 1955. According to this method, each person has four zones of different qualities:

Open - qualities known to us and acknowledged by others.

Hidden - qualities known to us but not known to others.

Blind - our qualities known to others but unknown to us.

Unknown - qualities that are known of no one, neither us nor others.

Continuously studying these 'windows' will allow us to get to know ourselves, develop our strengths, work on problematic areas, and remain an enthusiastic explorer of our own uncharted 'territory'.

> **Thirdly, it is essential to remember that any significant success is always made up of numerous successful small, seemingly unimportant tasks, challenges, and activities.**

Every success should be noticed and celebrated (you don't necessarily need to drink to that). These small victories significantly contribute to our self-confidence, conveying a priceless message to our subconscious mind: **'I can'**. Our good memory for victories and successes is formed out of these small successes and messages in our subconscious. As for our mistakes and failures, we begin to see them as valuable experiences.

> **Most importantly, start doing what you dream of or what you want to do as early as possible, without fear of potential failures, judgment, lack of understanding from others, or wrong decisions.**

There are no defeats on the path to happiness, confidence, and inner freedom. We either win or learn from our own and others' mistakes, gaining invaluable experience — experience that leads us to the heights of our dreams. Although a bit of luck wouldn't hurt either!

THE OBVIOUS IS UNBELIEVABLE

...And admiration for the creator,
Whose unknown envoy to us
With an unrecognizable face
In the most significant revelations,
And in the fleetest insights,
Gave judgment to every manifestation —
Everything is achieved through labor.

Alexander Pushkin

People of the older generation surely remember this popular science program from Soviet times with the irreplaceable Professor Sergey Petrovich Kapitsa as the host. At the very least, practically everyone remembers the opening sequence with the handwritten poem by the great Russian poet.

Many years later, I learned that there was one more line in this short poem, which the citizens of the USSR didn't necessarily need to know at the time.

The poem written by Alexander Pushkin in 1829 deserves our close attention even two centuries later. Here it is:

Oh, how many wondrous discoveries
Enlightenment prepares for our spirit,
And experience, the child of arduous errors,
And genius, the friend of paradoxes,
And chance, the inventive god...

I have always liked the great poet's works, possibly because of his light and flowing style. A significant factor was that Pushkin's poetry was easy to memorize regardless of its volume. In primary school, probably due to my curly hair and long nose, I had a relatively harmless nickname for a while - Pushkin, which lately frizzled out. It may have vanished after I seriously took up the sport, which was called classical back then.

I always loved the show 'the obvious is unbelievable', but I never thought about the fact that Pushkin was not even thirty when he wrote one of the greatest poems, in my opinion. Undoubtedly, brevity is the soul of wit, as said the doctor who became a famous writer and playwright, born thirty-one years after the emergence of this poem. There's no arguing with that. What interests me more is observing how the great poet, who became the founder of the Russian literary language, described his entire life in these five lines. This may be the shortest and most concise autobiography ever written by a person rightfully called a genius.

This isn't a literary journal, but for a teaser, I'll offer my interpretation of the first two lines of this 'autobiography'. From early childhood, 'our everything', as his elder sister Olga confirmed, 'was just a slacker' who found studying challenging. Teachers complained about his lack of diligence and lack of scholarly success. But everything changed when the future genius became passionate about READING. He 'spent sleepless nights secretly devouring one book after another in his father's study', as his younger brother Le remembered.

You can decipher the rest of the lines yourself by reading, perhaps more than once, the biography of the great poet, as I have done.

Perhaps such obvious 'ingredients' as reading, subsequent experience gained through catching frogs. your own bumps, breaking free from conventional thinking, and keenly observing accidentally (or not accidentally?) unfolding opportunities will help you progress along the path to the life of your unbelievable dreams.

SECRET TO SUCCESS

You can't control others, if you can't control yourself.

Proverb

Ever since I started writing my essays and posting them online, I've come across various attention-grabbing advertisements like 'Reveal the secrets of losing weight in one day', 'How to become a millionaire in one month', 'How to never work again and live on an island in the Caribbean', and so on and so forth.

From time to time, that's just how we're wired, each of us wants to become a fortunate character in some fairy tale or win the lottery. But statistically, the odds are not in our favor in that regard.

So, does the universally sought-after secret to success exist for each of us?

I have great news for you: it does. Furthermore, upon closer examination, it's not a secret.

Its name is self-discipline.

Self-discipline, when turned into a ritual or a specific sequence of actions that you regularly follow.

Actually, as a golfer, I'm much more inclined to use the English word 'routine', In day to day life it might have a somewhat gloomy connotation. In golf, it's precisely routine rituals that help distinguish a professional from an amateur almost instantly. The same goes for life.

Let's take a closer look at this. Every year, I assemble a small group of people. I help them achieve goals they have yet to gain the ability to reach on their own. Our collaboration always starts with a small test I've designed: five blocks of questions on five topics related to our fundamental needs, followed by a discussion of the results with potential participants in my mentoring program.

Based on the test results, conversations, and discussions, we developed an action plan to accomplish several tasks, with one main task always among them. Not two, not three, not ten, but ONE. Usually, it's a financial goal. By the way, my experience shows that many problems in our daily lives can often be easily remedied with a simple fix — money.

I want to clarify that all participants are educated, intelligent, innovative, and successful individuals in the conventional sense.

> **I assist them in formulating their dreams correctly, turning them into financial goals, and then working on achieving them with DISCIPLINE and conscious effort.**

Very often, we get stuck at the very first steps related to physiological aspects such as nutrition and hydration, proper sleep, necessary physical activity, and planning an optimal daily routine that should lead to an increase in energy levels, without which it is simply impossible to achieve desired results.

Remember the joke: 'What if there's a war, and I'm tired!'

The formation and development of a successful person start with the basics. You might be surprised, but if you can control your appetite, you can control any aspect of your life. Again, it's impossible without self-discipline.

It's self-discipline, going hand in hand with a well-formulated and intentional motivation, that helps achieve results in any endeavor, whether it's your health, personal or business relationships, making money, or realizing the most incredible dream.

BASIC MATHEMATICS

Achievement equals skills multiplied by effort. I really like this simple formula! It applies to any achievements in any field on a macro and micro level. From a sports team to a large company, from a brilliant musician to an average student, from an individual to an entire country. It may seem straightforward — just follow it, and success is guaranteed. However, as we know, simple doesn't mean easy.

Recently, I signed up for a golf tournament for participants over 50. Out of 184 participants, only 12 had a handicap under ten, approximately six and a half percent of the total participants. A handicap is a universal measure of a golfer's level or skill. The lower the handicap, the higher the player's level.

To the 'experienced mathematicians', I'll say that I intentionally simplified the situation, not considering dozens and hundreds of different parameters that explain why 172 people have not reached this level or have fallen from previous heights.

However, I contend that the skills possessed by these twelve individuals and the efforts they exerted to reach their current level are significantly better and higher than the 'average temperature in the hospital'.

They may have developed their skills many years ago and are simply enjoying their favorite game, slowly spending the capital they accumulated earlier. Or maybe they are just as 'crazy' as I am, starting their golf journey after the age of 30 and desperately trying to catch up with their peers who started earlier.

Each of us has skills that are unique to us. We have also made decisions in the past or are making them now on how much effort we are willing to put in to achieve our desired accomplishments.

I am sure that each of us has several real-life examples of how a talented but passive person buried their talents. And vice versa, an average person, from whom no one expected anything outstanding, made a brilliant career before our eyes.

The same applies to countries. There are hardly a dozen that we can designate as models to emulate in various areas. How well do they fit into our formula? A striking example here could be China, which, like a diligent student, learned from two superpowers over decades, slowly but surely accumulating the necessary skills that, almost unnoticed and unexpectedly to the world, multiplied with their efforts in the form of hard work and persistence in achieving their goals. Strategic vision, long-term planning, interconnected development programs at all levels, support for mass private entrepreneurship, and a healthy competitive environment also contribute to the country's advancement to the status of one of the world's leaders.

So, what hinders us from moving towards our intended achievements? Lack of necessary skills or an inability to make efforts at the right time?

I often see talented and intelligent people striving for perfection, continually refining their product, idea, or project, forgetting that they first need to put effort into getting the word out about themselves, their ideas, projects, or products to potential clients, investors, or employers first. In fact, I'm guilty of this myself!

On the other hand, we sometimes encounter highly active individuals who may currently lack subject knowledge. Still, they vigorously promote themselves, their ideas, and projects, acquiring the necessary expertise to do their work. Of course, one could argue that they should go and learn first. Without denying the importance of education, I advocate for the 'learning by doing' approach.

Our universal formula suggests that

> **Success can be achieved by super-talented individuals with exceptional skills and by persistent individuals willing to put in the effort to realize their goals.**

This applies to both individuals and entire countries.

ARE YOU READY FOR A BETTER LIFE?

The ability to courageously overcome oneself has always been one of the most outstanding achievements a rational person can be proud of.

Pierre de Beaumarchais

Over the course of many years of working in various fields, companies, and organizations, I have conducted thousands of interviews with people who wanted to work in these organizations or with me.

If the person is unfamiliar to me, I usually try to discern, beyond the standard information about their education, experience, or interests, the skills, abilities, potential, and the scale of the candidate's personality that are required by me or the organization I represent.

During the actual interview, which typically takes 40-45 minutes, I ask the candidate to tell me about themselves, their experience, and their interests. Very often, I hear almost everything that I have already read. But what is more important to me now is not what the person is saying but HOW they are talking about themselves, their previous experience, or hobbies. Their narrative helps me understand if the person can articulate their thoughts and how much time they need to cope with the natural nervousness in the first few minutes of an important meeting.

Of course, I ask questions, but primarily, I observe the speed and quality of the respondent's reactions. I take notice their emotional reactions and body language during our conversation. Obviously, questions usually vary depending on the industry, region, potential position of the applicant in the organization, age, interests, etc.

To cut to the chase, approximately one in ten candidates receives a job offer from me. And only one out of ten accepted candidates stayed with me for over a year. I have always considered this an excellent result for myself. On the other hand, it may be a clear indicator of competition.

There are two questions I always ask everyone. The first one is,

> **'Tell me, honestly, how much money do you need to be happy?'**

Practically inspired by Ilf and Petrov, when Ostap Bender asks Balaganov that question.

As a rule, most people respond pretty quickly. Over more than a quarter of a century, I have heard many answers to this question. And if I were to attempt a very rough generalization, the answer in most cases is approximately this: 'A million dollars. Heh-heh'.

Truth be told, the mentioned amounts are not crucial for me. How much a person ponders over the answer, how they name any sum, how serious or humorous they are about it — all of this allows me to understand how invested they are in creating and developing their most important 'business' — themselves.

> **A person capable of caring for themselves is much more likely to care for their loved ones than a 'collectivist', constantly seeking and successfully finding excuses for their learned helplessness.**

My second question always follows, as they say, in the same vein as the first:

| 'What are you willing to do to achieve it?'

Let me clarify that I'm referring to the efforts you are willing to actually PUT IN. Specifically, consistently apply effort, not just make a one-time effort to achieve financial happiness. How long and how systematically are you willing to do something that could help you achieve your goals?

As a rule, contemplating the answer to the second question takes more time. And this, too, is serious food for thought.

'For whom?' you might ask. For yourself, I'll answer! How many of you can right now, without hesitation, without smirks and doubts (saying, 'What's the difference? It won't work anyway!'), clearly and unequivocally answer these two straightforward questions for yourselves?

Everyone wants to believe that we deserve the best. But are we ready for a better life? Because if we don't bother to reflect in advance on such vital questions, what tune will we sing along the way? Of course, reflection requires effort, patience, and discipline. But I assure you, it's worth it!

After all, by contemplating these questions, you'll inevitably come face to face with... yourself!

Oh yes! Often, we don't really know ourselves. What are we good at? Do we prefer noisy gatherings or quietness? Where and how do we decompress best after work or stress? Going for drinks doesn't count. What will we do if suddenly we lose our job or business tomorrow? Will your profession still exist in 10 or 20 years? And dozens more questions.

And who knows, after such 'homework', you might not want to go to another interview. Or, on the contrary, it might help you find your dream job faster.

MAY GROUNDHOG DAY HELP YOU

*Every person is given at least ten daily opportunities
to change their life. Success comes to those who
know how to use them.*

André Maurois

Indeed, for those who have watched this fantastic movie with Bill Murray, the mention of it involuntarily brings a smile to our faces. As we remember, the plot revolves around the main character repeatedly experiencing the same day over and over again.

Despairing and resigned to this inevitability and tired of battling this new reality, our hero begins to take actions that might introduce some variety into his repeating days. I deliberately don't emphasize that of course (as is often the case in American cinema!), he performs only good deeds. Let's focus on the fact that he DOES perform these actions. In other words, HE ACTS.

So, what can all of us take from this iconic movie today? The older we get, the more inclined we are to fall into the trap of standard clichés like 'this isn't for me, I know myself, I can't do that, I won't succeed, others are better at this'.

These 'beliefs' possess an incredibly paralyzing power that only strengthens our convictions about ourselves, leading us into a whirlpool of self-disappointments, in people and sometimes in life itself.

And yet, very often, all you need to do is allow yourself to live without fearing to try everything, or at least something, from your 'I can't, I'm not able, it's not for me' list. After all, we did EVERYTHING for the first time at some point. Whether fearing or not fearing to fall, clumsily getting up, riding a bicycle or driving a car for the first time, having the first meeting with a client or a boss at a new job, skydiving. And thousands upon thousands of other things.

I am sure you probably have happy memories of most of these events. You can laugh, recall them, or relive the feeling of pride again because you still managed to do it despite your trembling hands or knees.

So, I'll repeat it once again:

| Allow. Yourself. To live.

Again, like when you were a child, trying and trying, getting scrapes and bruises, moving forward, crossing out one after another position from your 'I can't, I'm not able, it's not for me' list. Isn't this called stepping out of the comfort zone? But you didn't know about that when you were a kid, did you?

100 MILLION FOR EVERYONE

*A person truly values life only when they
have something infinitely more valuable
than their own life.*

Vasily Sukhomlinsky

Everything in this life comes at a price. I'm sure many of us not only have heard this statement but also experienced confirmations of it firsthand. Typically, we tend to see the 'price' as some sort of punishment for our wrongdoings, actions, or decisions.

However, I prefer a more comprehensive approach to this issue. After all, if we have something to pay for, then, by definition, we have the opportunity to do it. A successful bank or a functioning company has resources, assets, income, etc. We should look closer at ourselves as a business, understanding that no organization can afford to spend its resources paying numerous bills.

A good company should earn more than it spends, care about replenishing its treasury, and use these funds for dynamic, progressive development in the interests of customers, society, employees, owners, or shareholders. Then, what is the value of our own 'company' — our life?

Realizing I am treading on thin ice, I'll clarify immediately: I consider human life an absolute value. However, unfortunately, words uttered both with reason and without sometimes lose their original meaning for us.

At times, they turn into empty sounds, the true meaning of which reaches us too late. We cannot find our life path and lose friends, exciting jobs, and sometimes even a beloved person because we didn't value or invest effort, time, energy, or money but instead saved them. Or the opposite, live in the day, thoughtlessly squandering valuable resources, not realizing their actual value and worth.

I won't list various approaches and methods of evaluating human life here. Yet, until humanity abolishes money, my minimum estimate of the value of our own life-'company' is $100 million. By default, each of us. And here, every person is their own businessman or businesswoman.

Some go bankrupt, some barely make ends meet, some are well off, and others may make hundreds or billions.

> **But the principal meaning of an entrepreneur's life, just like an ordinary person's, is still not in money, but in stumbling and falling, getting up again and again, moving forward continuously, helping other people's companies', and the entire humanity with their experience.**

By the way, the first time I pondered the value of a life was over 40 years ago, back in the Soviet era, in a pioneer camp.

One day, they organized a kind of a fair for us, with swings, carousels, free souvenirs, fruits, sweets, kvass and soda under the slogan 'How much does free cost?' To explain to us that in economics, nothing is ever free. For every gingerbread, candy, souvenir, or chance to ride the carousel, you had to recite a poem, solve a riddle, tell a proverb.

My favorite and most fruitful 'tokens' were 'The further you get, the harder the going' and 'No pain, no gain'. I still remember the delicious taste of 'well-earned' chocolate gingerbread. The most important thing for me was that I already had, then, thanks to my parents, enough 'resources' in the form of various sayings, poems, and proverbs, to be able to afford to even 'give' them away to the other kids as what one might call charitable assistance nowadays.

We should treat ourselves as a multimillion-dollar company, nurturing, developing, and preserving it. Utilize the given body and mind, constantly explore and expand one's creative, physical, intellectual, and emotional potential to fully realize one's purpose. After all, this is what happiness is.

GOOD SALARY?

The world is made up of idlers who want money without working and idiots who are willing to work without getting rich.

George Bernard Shaw

For the older generation, a good salary is one of the measures of success in life. And for most people, a salary is synonymous with money.

Let's try to understand if this is really the case. Many of us, unable to grasp the essence of these concepts, have fallen and continue to fall into the trap of not understanding our potential.

More than twenty years ago, our four-year-old daughter asked, 'Tell me, Dad, are we rich?' I awkwardly attempted to explain to her what education, wealth, money, effort, risks, and opportunities were. But as I delved into the explanations, the eyes of my beloved little girl filled with tears. She finally burst into tears at the final sentence. 'Mom and I earned money for our home, for a good car, for beautiful things for ourselves and you with our hard, sometimes dangerous, work. So yes, many people consider us wealthy', I replied. 'So, does that mean we are bad, like all wealthy people?' she asked, crying.

The next half-hour was spent calming the crying child. I gave various examples, stories, and fairytales featuring 'good', wealthy people. Only a quote from Sergey Dovlatov's book finally put her at ease: 'Having a large salary allows one the luxury of kindness'.

IN MY OPINION, THERE ARE SEVERAL MAIN MODELS OF INTERACTING WITH MONEY

The first, the simplest one, is time in exchange for money.

The second, more effective, is time and knowledge in exchange for money.

The third, more 'advanced', is time, knowledge, and experience in exchange for money.

The fourth is time, knowledge, experience, and capital in exchange for money.

Capital can be diverse — financial, intellectual, emotional, and moral. However, a salary should serve the purpose of drawing your attention to some problem, task, topic, or phenomenon.

Numerous studies show that money actively influences our brain and nervous system. This effect is sometimes comparable in its impact to that of a drug. You have probably noticed how different your attitude is towards services or items that you've purchased compared to those obtained for free.

> **Those for which we paid, especially with hard-earned money, are usually more valuable to us.**

Therefore, a salary acts as a 'magic pill', helping negotiating parties concentrate attention on each other. The active attention of an employer can assist you in showcasing your skills and abilities more vividly, demonstrating enthusiasm and persistence in achieving set goals. You are no longer indifferent to them; they pay you money, so it's time for you to move forward without hesitation or delay.

> **After all, attention, just like money, is not limitless.**

Attention is, in fact, money.

Your customers' attention can spot your service or product amidst the hail of daily advertising messages. The attention of your employer, recognizing you as a prospective employee or manager. The attention of a potential investor, choosing your company from dozens or hundreds of similar organizations. The attention of your lover, observing unique qualities in you as an ideal life companion.

Therefore, attention is the magical tool for your future prosperity and success.

ARE YOU IDLING? WELL DONE!

I'm never as busy as I am during my leisure hours.

Cicero

When people talk about rest, they traditionally divide into two opposing camps. Some believe that we rest too much, while others think the opposite. I belong to the latter. I rest always, everywhere, and at the first opportunity.

I generally consider myself lazy, although my family and those who have worked or are working with me might disagree. Undoubtedly, every person is unique, and therefore, each requires a different time for recovery after physical, intellectual, and especially emotional stress. This primarily applies to intellectual labor specialists and managers. After a workday, they simply can't 'shut the door' in their heads, continuing to mentally replay the day's events. For example, they prepare for an important meeting or conference the next day. I relate to them! I'm just like that.

Unfortunately, we're not getting any younger. Each year, we need more and more time to recover from the same stresses. Often, ignoring this simple fact leads to 'unexpected' illnesses or premature death at the peak of one's powers. Burned out at work.

How many of those silent 'torches' wander through the expanses of the corporate

| world?

The minimum required rest for an intellectual worker includes two weeks of winter holidays, two weeks of spring break, three months in the summer, and two weeks in the fall. I would add a four-day workweek to this. Additionally, considering modern means of communication, one could avoid.

Showing up to work in person if the employer is satisfied. I can hear the whistling of rotten eggs and tomatoes flying in my direction.

Okay-okay! Let's talk about labor productivity. In most companies and organizations, the culture of 'being present' rather than 'getting things done' still prevails. Unfortunately, the desire to control everything and the flourishing micromanagement do not contribute to productivity development; on the contrary, they reduce it.

It's helpful to ask ourselves: 'Why do I go to work to accomplish something or feel needed or indispensable? Am I coming to the office to work or to socialize? How much does the overall result depend on me? Do I fully understand my tasks for today, this month, and this year? Do I know how much time I spend working, excluding breaks and coffee?'

Let's admit that many of us enjoy being needed, awaited, and considered indispensable.

The truth? Delegation is the flip side of trust. And most of us have issues with that.

WE. DON'T. TRUST. ANYONE.

The perfect employee for me is someone to whom you can assign a task and forget about it and the worker. At least, I've always strived for this, and 'heroic' tales about who, why, and where someone went on a metaphorical bus to fulfill a task were never appreciated. But the perfect employee also needs a perfect manager who doesn't hinder their work. Not someone who always tries with an intelligent look, invariably in a white coat, to touch a cow's udder and doesn't allow the cow or the milker to do their job. Understanding what a manager shouldn't do could significantly increase productivity and foster mutual trust. This is where the problems of low productivity lie.

Returning to the theme of relaxation, I'll say that relaxation for the soul is as important as a growth hormone for the body. It isn't produced during workouts, but when we sleep, making us stronger, healthier, and more alert.

It's precisely during down time that we and our brains have the necessary time to 'digest' valuable and essential information, which we sometimes simply can't process in haste and turmoil.

Relaxation actually reduces the time required for any work, especially for complex tasks.

Allowing us to enjoy our favorite hobbies, time spent with family, or a book. A healthy, rested, emotional intellect can drive personal and professional development, from which your business or company will only benefit.

ABSOLUTE HAPPINESS

I would of loved to tell you that I often get asked about self-actualization, pause significantly, gaze at the sky, and slowly begin this challenging conversation.

But alas. I don't hear this question often. It's not surprising Because most people are engaged in their daily battles, in their own physiology and safety, sense of belonging, and respect. Some haven't managed let alone self-actualization, a level that, according to the opinions of numerous eminent psychologists of the present and past centuries, such as Kazimierz Obuchowski, Gordon Allport, Abraham Maslow, and many others, only about one percent of the Earth's population will attain.

Besides the approaches of Maslow, whom I admire, I resonate with the ideas of Gordon Allport, the initiator of the development of the systemic approach to studying personality. He believed that

Our personality is an open and evolving psychophysiological system, the core of which is the human 'self'.

The distinct feature of this system is the individual's inclination towards realizing their life potential towards self-actualization.

So, what is this 'beast'? I am convinced that self-actualization is the peak of personal development, helping us become increasingly mature individuals. After all, a fulfilled person is, primarily, a developed personality who realizes their potential to the fullest extent at the edge of their capabilities. It is someone who constantly grows and expands their scope to fully realize their potential in all spheres of their life aspirations and needs.

For those interested in their own progress along the path of self-actualization, I strongly recommend reading the original article by A. Maslow[1], which he wrote based on a study he conducted in collaboration with E. Rashevsky and D. Friedman at one of the American colleges. By the way, out of three thousand people, Maslow initially selected only ONE student who was somewhat suitable for his research on mature personality.

[1] - A. Maslow. Motivation and Personality. Moscow: Peter, 2019. - Part 3. Self-Actualization.

THE MAIN FEATURES OF A MATURE PERSONALITY WERE RECOGNIZED AS FOLLOWS:

Effective perception of reality and comfortable relationships with it.

Self-acceptance, acceptance of others, and nature.

Spontaneity, simplicity, and naturalness.

Service.

Detachment and a need for solitude.

Independence, cultural independence, will, and potency.

A fresh perspective on things.

Mystical and higher experiences.

Sense of community.

Deep interpersonal relationships.

Democratism.

Ability to distinguish means from ends and good from evil.

Philosophical sense of humor.

Creativity.

Resistance to cultural influences and transcendence of culture (oh, how!).

These qualities undoubtedly deserve a separate conversation, which we will continue.

By the way, Maslow and his colleagues could find only a few dozen historically known figures who, partly or fully, could fit the description of a mature personality.

I was lucky; life brought me into contact with several such individuals. One of them happened to be involved in my birth — my father.

The second person is the legendary musician, cellist, pianist, composer, conductor, educator, and public figure Mstislav Rostropovich, jokingly calling himself Slavka, literally forcing me and all his friends to call him Slava and use the informal 'you' regardless of the age difference and other formalities. He even had a kind of jokey ritual for transitioning to the casual 'you', which included a mandatory lover's toast, after which it was necessary to brush off formalities and go informal. The logic of the great artist was ironclad — how could one be formal after that?

Here, you have simplicity, a philosophical sense of humor, democratization, independence, self-acceptance, acceptance of others, and many other traits in one shining package.

10 RULES FOR A HAPPY LIFE

Many years ago, already being a decent golfer, I discovered books by the well-known American psychologist Bob Rotella and his 'Ten Rules of the Perfect Round'.[2] These rules are surprisingly simple. They work excellently if you are patient enough to integrate them into your routine just as many stars of the global sports world, particularly golf, have done. But as Rotella himself says,

It's simple, but not easy.

Today, I know them by heart, but this rule book is always in my golf bag. Before every important competitive round, I reread them to activate my visual memory and not forget about them in the heat of my beloved game, which has captivated me for over 25 years. Because, as boxing enthusiasts know, everyone has a plan until they get punched in the jaw. Perhaps golfers will understand me better. And for those who haven't yet dabbled in golf, just take my word for it: golf is a game, closest to the game called life.

> **You get a good result from bad shots, a bad result from good shots, but you must play from where your ball lands.**
> **That's what the legendary golfer Bobby Jones said.**

Easier said than done.

After I started using these rules in golf, I noticed that I often refer to them when offering advice to my loved ones, friends, and acquaintances before essential events in their lives, such as exams, unpleasant

² - www.golfdigest.com/story/rotella

meetings, personal relationships, when making decisions about their career development, leaving government service, or potentially transitioning to working in a major company. Observing and contemplating how these rules operate in everyday life, I formulated my own rules for life, which gradually transformed into rules for a happy life.

HERE THEY ARE:

1. Live to live a great life , not just to not live poorly.

2. Love the challenge of the day, whatever it may be.

3. Don't dwell on the outcome. Immerse yourself in the process.

4. Know that nothing will upset you today, and you'll be in a great mood throughout the day.

5. Living with a mindset where the outcome doesn't matter is almost always preferable to worrying too much.

6. Believe in yourself — and you'll be able to live freely.

7. Clearly envision what you want to achieve.

8. Be decisive, precise, and straightforward.

9. Be your own best friend.

10. Strive for balance in everything.

The tenth rule on my personal list periodically changes depending on the stage of my life. I ultimately borrowed some of the rules from my colleague Rotella (I hope he doesn't mind). I'll immediately clarify that he probably has no idea about it, but it doesn't hurt to take this opportunity to thank him for the suggestions. Others I adapted and modified. They may help you too.

It might be hard to believe, but these rules help every day, not just me, move toward achieving any person's primary goal — happiness. After all, happy people make the world a better place. Let's do it together!

RULE #1

Live to live a great life, not to not live poorly

*All our dreams can come true if we
dare to pursue them.*

Walt Disney

For as long as I can remember, I've always had big dreams. Some of the very first were:

- A pedal-powered toy car, 'Moskvich-401'.

- Marrying my older sister's classmate

- Becoming a cosmonaut

- A battery-operated toy chef who expertly flipped eggs in a frying pan

- A pack of 'Laika' brand cigarettes

- And others

As a little boy, I was persistent, so all my dreams turned into goals that I pursued, as it seemed to me then, in a confident manner, constantly adjusting them... And the list of actual 'dreams' itself was not a fixed form.

As I grew taller, the pedal car was inevitably excluded from my list because my knees were jamming into the dashboard, and I couldn't extend my long legs toward the coveted pedals. Feeling down, I replaced the car with a splendid jigsaw set with a satellite on the box and shifted my focus to my sister's classmate.

As I understand now, she was an older girl, about nine years old. Her name was Nelly. She smelled nice, had beautiful lace cuffs on her school uniform, and I loved sitting on her lap. In short, I was a step away from marriage, which I announced to my parents.

After hearing me out and retraining from laughing (a huge thanks to them for this and much more), they approved my choice with a severe expression, stating that according to the law, I had to wait until I got my passport before embarking on this journey.

I didn't become a cosmonaut; the toy chef lost his relevance, but a few cigarettes (I already had an empty pack by then) were obtained by direct blackmail (refusing to go to kindergarten) from my sister, who was running late for school. The joy was short-lived because, after twenty minutes, the cigarettes were confiscated using the same tactic I had employed, by my sister, right before entering kindergarten.

As I matured, all my dreams grew, changed, and evolved, acquiring details and nuances. Some dreams made it to the list of fulfilled dreams. New dreams emerged, painting a constantly moving picture of a bright future - a magnificent bright future that takes your breath away and makes your heart beat faster at the mere thought of it.

Unfortunately, many people are afraid to dream, not understanding or forgetting about the main thing amidst their daily problems: no dream, no goal. You got no goal — essentially, you're the Flying Dutchman, sailing into the unknown. Certainly not towards the magnificent life of your dreams.

Life is balanced when dreams become concrete goals, which become the foundation for plans. After all, our dreams help us create the future — an exhilarating future that gains more apparent outlines with each passing year, transforming into the present in which we live every day. We live to live a great life.

RULE #2

Love the challenge of the day, whatever it may be

If you stopped facing difficulties, it means you've strayed from the path.

— Unknown author

This is one of my most essential and favorite rules. I prefer the word 'challenge' because, besides its literal meaning, it also signifies a problem or a complex task. So, my rule in a more elaborate form reads:

> **'Love any challenge, any complex task, any problem, whatever they may be'.**

For the unprepared, this statement might seem strange or even daunting. However, upon reflection, we'll realize that our lives are an uninterrupted sequence of challenges, problems, and complex tasks we encounter almost every minute.

The first words or independent steps of a rapidly growing child, the first solved math or physics problem in school, the first adolescent date or kiss. Excelling in a graduation or entry exam, answers written down with the hands trembling from nervousness.

The first day at your dream company, the first independent flight in a jet plane, the first significant contract, or the first paragraph of the book you dreamed of writing but hesitated to start, overwhelmed with hundreds of doubts and excuses.

You can continue this list with thousands of examples of 'unsolvable' problems and challenges. They were unsolvable until you solved them.

Perhaps you were scared, with shaky knees, sweat beading on your forehead, or a sneaky trickle down your back. It doesn't matter. If only we knew how many great deeds, discoveries, accomplishments, or heroic acts were carried out in such a state.

In the early '90s, my beautiful wife, who had graduated from a conservatory in vocal studies (mezzo-soprano, if you're wondering) and moved to Moscow with me, was offered a modeling job at one of the rapidly growing foreign companies. In the massive hall of the company's flagship store, fashion shows were held every hour, presenting collections for sale. This job promised to be a breath of fresh air for my wife, who was lost in the impossibility of her creative realization. It was challenging for many Soviet people to find their place in the new country.

The stage was a familiar place for a professional opera singer. But it turned out that walking quickly in 15-centimeter heels, following various interaction patterns with colleagues on the runway, was much more challenging than it might seem to an inexperienced spectator. The first words wife uttered, terrified of putting on her brand new patent leather stilettos, were, 'No! I will never walk in these!'

Then came the first timid steps, holding hands with me on the tattered rug in our one-bedroom apartment on the outskirts of Moscow. After that, the first independent steps, the first turn, the first change of direction.

The cramps that brought tears and sleepless nights, and an array of other 'pleasant' details, including a diet of just one apple and one cup of yogurt per day, and much more.

Nearly 30 years later, many of those 'unsolvable' problems have faded into obscurity. But I am certain that these problems and difficulties also became crucial steps on her path to creating and designing her own brand of clothing and jewelry. This, in turn, logically led her to creative heights as an artist, exhibiting and selling her artworks worldwide.

Love the challenge of the day, whatever it may be! Who knows, perhaps these are the first steps towards your bright present and future.

RULE #3

Don't dwell on the result.
Immerse yourself in the process

*Start there. Take baby steps. You don't need
passion to succeed. Do what you do with love
and success is a natural symptom.*

James Altucher

My readers continuously strive toward the peaks of their personal growth and success. Those who can articulate a description for their short-term and long-term aspirations, turning them into goals. And goals become tasks they tackle daily, bringing their grand plans to life.

And for those who haven't done this yet, don't be disheartened! Grab pens, pencils, and paper, and start compiling a list of what your heart desires.

Let's assume that each of us can clearly imagine the ideal possible result of an action, process, occupation, or deed. For instance, speaking of athletes, such a result could be winning a tournament, setting a world or personal record, finishing a game with a particular score, and much more.

For an entrepreneur, it could be closing a profitable deal, attracting a specific investment, or achieving the desired sales volume within a given timeframe. What unites them all is that professionals know and understand what it is that they want to achieve clearly.

Now, let's talk about the process. You might be surprised, but the attention to the process distinguishes professionals from amateurs. In any endeavor! The result often lies beyond our control. However, when our mind focuses on the actions we can control, these actions lead us to theshot in the final moments of a Champions League match. From a well-structured lecture to preparing a favorite dish. From skillfully conducted meetings with investors to routine conversations with clients. In all these situations,

> **The result is a byproduct of a well-organized process,**

those mundane actions that you have mastered and consistently repeat in all the 'practice' matches, games, lectures, client or investor meetings.

> **Moreover, routine becomes your reliable companion in the most crucial moments, subtly signaling, 'Relax, you've done this thousands of times. Go ahead, you can do it!'**

Understanding and structuring your processes, practicing them daily, and optimizing and refining them in high stakes situations will instill self-confidence in your subconscious — confidence in your strengths, abilities, and skills. It's precisely the steps repeated day after day that will lead you to results in any field, results that you can take pride in, whether it's in physiology, safety, involvement, or respect. From there, achieving self-realization becomes a reachable goal!

RULE #4

Know that nothing will upset you today, and you'll be in a great mood throughout the day

Every day of our lives confronts us with dozens and hundreds of different events, situations, messages, and news. I deliberately used the word 'confronts' to emphasize the unexpected nature of such events and situations. Not to mention the news. Today, we are forced to consume an enormous amount of information that even our evolving brain, developed over millions of years, cannot process adequately.

All of this leads to unconscious tension, which, over time, is exacerbated by the constant expectation of unpleasant and sometimes downright ominous news. We transfer our anxious state onto our loved ones and colleagues at work. The feeling of depletion of energy or mood swings becomes habitual. After all, our brains are designed so that negative information or experiences trigger a more vigorous response in our bodies than positive emotions. This is how nature (or evolution) ensured the survival of our prehistoric ancestors so that they wouldn't inadvertently ignore the appearance of a saber-toothed tiger or another predator while on a hunt.

But surely each of us has a friend or coworker who seems to live in a completely different world. They're positive and in a good mood. They always have a cheerful stori or kind words of support for anyone. Admit it, we sometimes envy such people with benign envy, wondering where they get their optimism from. 'That's just his character', we say as if acknowledging some inherent quality we want to possess. Isn't that so?

But what is character? Plutarch, an ancient Greek historian, moralist, biographer, writer, and philosopher who lived almost 2000 years ago, said:

| 'Character is simply a long-standing habit'.

If it's a habit, why don't we develop it in ourselves? Many years ago, I played pretty well in one of the golf tournaments in the first two days, leading the tournament before the final day of competition. The scores were close enough, so a riveting final round was ahead. I had frequently played with two of my flight partners in various tournaments, but it was the first time I had encountered the third opponent.

Somewhere in the middle of the round, I asked my new opponent to adhere to the commonly accepted rules of golf etiquette, which he had ignored several times before my eyes. My request may have sounded like a remark. Or the zeal for victory combined with a hefty dose of a well-known male hormone provoked a vehement reaction.

The aggressive rejection of any comments also triggered my emotional response. It led to a verbal skirmish between two adult men. To our credit, it didn't escalate to personal attacks. However, 'digesting' that situation, I made several regrettable mistakes on the following holes, missing the victory that had been so close.

One of my friends won the tournament, wisely refraining from involvement in the incident.

At that time, I didn't know this rule. But that situation prompted me to delve more deeply into the psychological aspects of golf, which subsequently led to creating my own rules for a happy and successful life.

Every morning while brushing my teeth, I mentally (and sometimes out loud) repeat a simple statement: 'Know that nothing will upset you today, and you'll be in a great mood throughout the day'. This simple practice has helped me secure more than one victory since then. And not just on the golf course.

RULE #5

Life with a mindset that the result doesn't matter is almost always preferable to worrying too much

If you find yourself in the dark and see even the faintest ray of light, you should go toward it instead of pondering whether it makes sense to do so or not.

Victor Pelevin

There's this funny word — 'kakorraphiophobia'. Have you heard of it? But I'm sure that almost everyone has faced what this tongue twister of a term describes at least once. Ka-ko-rra-phi-o-pho-bi-a. Simply put, it's the fear of failure.

It might seem that this fear is inherent in novices and various underachievers. No! You'll be surprised, but success-oriented people, sometimes referred to as high achievers, also suffer from this phobia. And not just in school.

And since we're talking about rules here, let's reflect on what comes to mind when we hear the word 'rules'. Game, quiz, raffle, competition. Competition in the broadest sense, from entry exams to college or university to job interviews for that coveted position in a large organization.

> **Our life is an engaging game where the result primarily depends on the desires, intentions, efforts, and professionalism of the players, which is us.**

Furthermore, it's impossible to lose in this game if you understand its relatively simple rules.

> **The most important of which states that you can either win the game, or learn something.**

And by learning something, we increase our chances of winning in the following 'round', 'period', or 'time'.

But you can lose in one and only one way — by exiting the game.

> **If you continue to play, making one attempt after another, you're already a winner regardless of the result. What's more, you are also your own referee, judge, and arbiter in this game.**

Unfortunately, the mass media, often addressing their own agendas, tend to focus our attention solely on the external aspect — the results.

We're always very interested in who won a football match or a golf tournament, how much money a well-known entrepreneur made, or how many followers a particular famous person has on social media.

> **Actual victories are often invisible to most external observers — fans, colleagues, partners, or clients.**

About 15 years ago, unexpectedly, I found myself in the hospital. After the examination, it turned out that urgent surgery was needed. At that time, besides my primary, reasonably demanding job, I oversaw organizing and preparing for Cyprus's first ever Russian Spring Golf Cup.

Hoping for an excellent sporting outcome was something I had to say goodbye to since a certain amount of time was required for recovery after the anesthesia and the surgery. My goal, my ideal outcome at that time, was simply to participate in the tournament. It was almost like acquiring the status of being an Olympian!

I won't delve into the nuances of my recovery program. I did take part in the competition! I can't even remember what place I ended up with; it doesn't matter. What matters is that it was a real victory for me. I enjoyed every minute spent on the emerald field. I savored each of my shots, even the not-so-great ones, simply reveling that I could somehow continue the game. A game in which I cannot lose as long as I'm playing.

RULE #6

Believe in yourself - and you will be able to live freely

The full version of this rule goes:

> **'Fully believe in yourself - and you will be able to live freely, without fears and prejudices'.**

One of the most essential qualities parents can instill in their children is confidence. It's the most crucial quality. Unfortunately, not everyone is as lucky with their parents as I was.

I'm also confident that reading and education have always been and will continue to be our allies in achieving goals and solving problems in various fields.

Speaking of confidence and prejudices, I must note that perhaps there is not a more dangerous combination than a confident fool. By the way, according to the Italian historian-economist Carlo Cipolla, it's the fools who pose the greatest threat to humanity.

> **According to Cipolla, fools are always in surplus. They are irrational and create problems for others practically without benefiting themselves.**

Back in 1993, my driving instructor wasn't acquainted with the works of the University of California's Berkeley professor, who wrote an essay about the five laws of human stupidity. However, the universal rule - 'Give way to the fool', that he taught me, is applicable practically everywhere.

Confidence is inseparable, oddly enough, from fear. It's precisely fear that prevents us from being truly free individuals. Surprisingly, many people cannot even dream without fear. When finally embarking on ambitious plans, people start to experience fear of failure at the slightest serious obstacle. It becomes a fear that engulfs all their thoughts and feelings, becoming a chilling, almost primal terror.

A notable statement attributed to Ambrose Redmoon goes: 'Courage is not the absence of fear, but the realization that something else can be much more important than fear'.

> **Your dreams (real dreams, not just wishes) can and should become something else, which is far more important than fear. The answers to the questions such as, 'Why? How?' 'What for?' will help you paint a brighter, more meaningful picture of your future.**

This vision will fill you up with energy. This energy, in turn, will fuel your self-assurance. This confidence will free you from fear, unlock your unlimited potential, and help you reach new heights.

RULE #7

Clearly envision what you want to achieve

Even if there's talent —
To not disrupt, not disappoint,
To not destroy, but to build, <...>
You need a very precise plan.

Vladimir Vysotsky. Alice in Wonderland

I've always thought this is one of the simplest and most comprehensible rules. However, the longer I work with people, the clearer it becomes that it's not entirely true. Especially considering the full version of this rule:

> **'Clearly envision what and when you want to achieve before your actions and undertakings'.**

It might seem that only a couple of words were added. Yet, these words help to determine where habit ends and conscious planning begins. I often talk about how each of us lives the life we dream of. At first, many people start to argue, sincerely not realizing that, in essence, they live by habit.

This rule is most fitting to apply when we start something new, a new task, or a project. We reflect and reason regarding deadlines, paces, and volumes at such times. The same applies to a new job, position, and sometimes even new relationships.

After a couple of months, and sometimes even earlier, we find ourselves again in the **familiar** cycle of events, actions, or emotions. The intensity of our attention, motivation, excitement, readiness, and joyful enthusiasm decreases to the mundane, requiring no extra effort. Consequently, progress toward the goal slows down.

If you feel that I am claiming to be perfect and infallible, let me point out that I use these rules as reminders **to myself**, to avoid falling into life's traps amidst routine chores and concerns. However, these hints will benefit everyone, both creative individuals and those caught in the quagmire of monotony or hopelessness.

Each of my readers wants to be happy, healthy, and wealthy. This is an excellent starting point for brainstorming and filling these desires with specific plans, deadlines, and responsible executors.

Think, then write down all your goals in these crucial directions: happiness, health, and wealth. Don't be afraid. Paper is patient!

> **To begin, create a 'draft' of your dream life so that you can regularly rewrite, supplement, improve, and amend it. Until you achieve the goals written there. Celebrate for a day — then create the new plan!**
>
> **You must constantly see the goal ahead of you; otherwise, the process will slip out of your control and become routine.**

Recently, while sorting through stacks of my old daily planners, I came across a page titled 'How I Want to Live. Questions', written by my hand many years ago. On the second page, I saw 'How I Want to Live. Answers'. Judging by the fact that the first sheet was written in blue ink and the second in black, I pondered for some time.

With your permission, I'll keep the first five points to myself. But I'll share the rest. The last three questions contained tasks for me.

HERE THEY ARE:

> 1. *Define what success means to me.*
>
> 2. *Define what wealth means to me/us.*
>
> 3. *What happiness means to me.*

I have the answers to these questions. Perhaps you'll be surprised, but these notes have not lost their relevance even now. I am living just as I once formulated in that old notebook.

RULE #8

Be decisive, clear, and mindful

> *The confidence which we have in ourselves gives birth to much of that, which we have in others.*
>
> *François de La Rochefoucauld*

I repeat this rule even more often than once a day.

By the way, all the rules are written succinctly for a very simple purpose - so that they are easy to remember. But if we decide to dig deeper, the full version of this rule sounds like this:

> **'Be clear and mindful in your thoughts — then you'll be decisive in your actions and deeds'.**

The road to happiness, success, wealth, and self-realization always begins with a dream. Some people were luckier than others: life made them move, placing them in unbearable conditions. After all, life is our best teacher. Very often in the biographies of famous people, we read that they were famished, homeless, their father or mother were alcoholics, or the parents died, and the hero was the fifth or tenth child in the family. Sounds scary?

But these terrible events or circumstances helped them form clear and mindful ideas **about the kind of life they didn't want for themselves**.

And then they were able to direct their energy, their will

> **Towards their dream life, sometimes subconsciously trying to make it so bright that the terrible flashes from their past were not visible in the light of this new shining life.**

Another much more challenging path is motivation through achievements. Each of us tends to be lazy, sometimes burying our talent in the ground, using previous generations' money, knowledge, property, or achievements of our own families, and of the humanity as a whole. Determination and achievements in favorable circumstances are much more valuable in my system of coordinates. These people could consciously break out of their comfort zone in the literal sense of the word. And that's a challenging task.

> **But they had a dream, an idea that drove them forward, regardless of anything.**

It doesn't matter what motivations guided representatives of both groups.

> **What matters is that they knew what they wanted (or didn't want).**

Did they make mistakes along the way? Of course. Did they fill their own bruises and bumps? Absolutely! But every mistake, bump, or bruise was a necessary price for success. It only added value and significance to their achievements. And it served as a cue for those who wanted to replicate their success. With their example, they seem to say, 'Anything is possible!'

Over 50 years ago, the Soviet Union led the space race. On February 3, 1966, the Luna-9 automatic station made a soft landing on the surface of the Moon.

Few know that, at that time, there were two different hypotheses about the Moon's surface. Thomas Gold's hypothesis claimed that the Moon was covered with a thick layer of cosmic dust, in which any landing apparatus would simply sink.

Head Developer Sergei Korolev, on the contrary, supported Soviet volcanologist Genrikh Shteinberg's idea that the Moon's surface was solid. But assumptions are one thing, and tremendous responsibility and determination are quite another in real life. And then Sergei Pavlovich, confident in his correctness, took a notebook and wrote boldly:

'The Moon is solid'.

This is a stunning example of confidence in one's beliefs, in one's path, in one's worldview.

Be clear and distinct in your thoughts — then you'll be decisive in your actions and deeds. Know what you want, have no doubts about yourself, and move towards your goal.

RULE #9

Be your own best friend

> *'If you want to meet someone who can fix any situation you don't like, who can bring you happiness in spite of what other people say or believe, look in a mirror, then say this magic word: 'Hello'.*
>
> *Richard Bach*

This is one of my favorite rules I tirelessly repeat to myself, my loved ones, my friends, and my clients. In response, I often hear questions and remarks like 'How can you live without friends?'. Everybody needs friends, and the like. I don't disagree. Moreover, I fully agree with this.

It's wonderful if you can seek advice from friends, parents, children, partners, work colleagues, or mentors at any time of each day.

But sometimes, I would say quite often, situations arise when there is no such opportunity for various reasons. It could be individual training or competition, a business trip or journey, an important meeting or exam, an accident, or an illness.

There are also moments when it seems like friends and loved ones are around, but burdening them with your problems and worries feels uncomfortable.

Because, we assume, they are swamped with their own problems and concerns, and here we come with our 'load' This leads to a person feeling lonely, often causing the destruction of relationships, friendships, families, or partnerships.

We all need someone to occasionally support us, give advice, or simply understand us silently. My rule allows you to talk to your best friend anytime, in any situation, 24 hours a day, seven days a week, 365 days a year. Leap year is no exception!

I'm absolutely sure that my best friend is always ready to listen to me. He is educated and experienced enough that I can trust him. He is emotionally stable and financially independent. He knows the members of my family, my clients, my partners, and all of my friends and acquaintances very well.

I firmly believe that he will never judge or gossip about me to anyone, so I can confidently share my most intimate thoughts, dreams, goals, plans, and desires with him.

Furthermore, becoming your own best friend is incredibly easy! Just start talking to yourself as if you were talking to a beloved, clever, beautiful, intelligent, educated, and mature person - someone who will always listen to you with gratitude, without interrupting or doubting a single word you say, because they are absolutely confident that you are acting in their best interest.

I don't know how it works, but by becoming my best friend, I've become a more empathetic and reliable friend to my loved ones, family, and those around me.

Became a more understanding senior comrade for my colleagues at work and those I mentor, helping them achieve their ambitious goals in various fields.

I sincerely hope that after you read this, you'll gain one more friend. The best friend.

RULE #10

Strive for balance in everything

> *Life is like riding a bicycle.*
> *To keep your balance, you must keep moving.*
>
> *Albert Einstein*

In our busy, sometimes chaotic life, numerous common phenomena, actions, events, words, and definitions exist.

We learn some words and their meanings in early childhood. However, there are times when their true significance, despite appearing obvious, isn't universally understood. We perceive certain phenomena differently based on the events we observe, and depending on our life experiences, years lived, or situations encountered, our perspectives toward seemingly identical things can be fundamentally different.

This rule is strategically important in my list. So, without theory, it can't be passed over. Oxford Languages, which has been compiling and publishing authoritative dictionaries in over 50 languages globally for over 150 years, provides us with several definitions of balance.

Physical: 'A state of rest in which a body is subjected to equal and opposite forces that cancel each other out'.

As I wrote this, I remembered my first childhood bicycle. It was turquoise-blue in color, with an adjustable saddle, front and rear brakes, a coveted bell on the handlebars, and two plastic training wheels that made the bicycle a four-wheeler. I immediately demanded to remove those wheels because I thought my bike would look more badass without them.

I didn't know that word then, but I wanted to look more grown-up, at four years old. There was a cool carrier rack on the rear wheel, where I planned to give rides to my elder sister, who sometimes helped me in my attempts to learn to ride independently. The only thing I didn't like about the new bicycle was the name 'Butterfly', which seemed a bit girlish to me then.

After almost fifty years, I can't accurately recall how long it took me to learn to maintain balance. But that moment when, to my surprise, I suddenly caught my balance, I remember vividly and in minor detail to this day.

Joyful fright, amazement, admiration, delight, and the desire to show off my new skill are some of the emotions of a little boy who just became a bit more independent.

Overall, it was one of the moments of bright and absolute happiness from the most ordinary physical phenomenon called balance.

As I grew, I replaced the 'Butterfly' with the 'Eaglet', then the 'Schoolboy', and then the 'Ural', which marked the end of my fascination with bicycles when it was stolen from where I left it next to my neighbourhood grocery store.

New interests, tasks, hobbies, sports, education, work, and family emerged. Moving to Moscow. Dorm room, rental apartment. The first apartment of my own. A new house. My daughter was born. Parents passed away...

And today, as perhaps for you as well, it's not only the direct and physical meaning of the word 'balance' that interests me.

Emotional: 'A state of calmness, equilibrium, absence of significant fluctuations in moods and relationships'.

It seems simple. But simple, as we remember, does not equal easy. And here, it's impossible to avoid reflecting on one's potential. Even such seemingly big words as destiny or mission would be entirely appropriate. Because a person with a mission acquires an image, outlining their bright and inspiring future. A future towards which they strive, regardless of the bumps and difficulties along the way. A future that helps to develop and expand existing opportunities for fully realizing one's potential in all spheres of life's aspirations and needs.

Physiology and safety, respect and empathy, self-realization, and self-actualization. Simply put, balance within each sphere and between them gives us a wonderful sense of happiness that we can and should learn to achieve.

EPILOGUE

At first, I wanted to cite only the first passage — 'The traveler will overcome the road' — as an epigraph for the epilogue. But then I thought that sometimes the negative, and sometimes even the scary side of our inaction, can be more motivating than the positive. Do you agree?

I think each of us has wanted to go back in time at least once and give ourselves a shake for laziness, passivity, and inaction. That's normal. Also, anyone can accidentally step on a rake. The main thing is not to turn it into a daily routine.

So how do we learn to balance, become our best friends, and happy, healthy and wealthy? How do we develop and expand our capabilities to fully realize our potential in all spheres of our life goals and aspirations? How do we help ourselves proactively and mindfully formulate and analyze our dreams? How do we turn them into goals and tasks? How do we independently set our path to success, freedom, confidence, and happiness?

Hints to all these questions are found in the book you are holding. After all, you probably guessed that none of my my stories are actually about drawing a pig or writing a greeting card for a holiday. They aren't fairy tales about a village idiot or physics lessons for high school students.

They're about how happiness has a structure to it, how for every complex problem, there are not just causes but also solutions if you don't give up, that you are the blacksmith of your own happiness. And an actual blacksmith doesn't just hit the anvil with a hammer. They know exactly what they will do, what materials and tools they need, and how much help, time, and effort it will take to complete a particular task.

This book is about being healthy and wealthy, being busy yet finding time to help others, working diligently, and indulging in leisure. It's about loving life and people, those close to us and strangers. It's about believing in ourselves and discovering our talents. It's about not waiting for help from others but accepting it gratefully when needed. It's about patience and the ability to act quickly and decisively.

About the ability to dream and turn our wildest dreams into specific goals and plans. And then to achieve them, regardless of the skepticism of the people around us, friends, or family. It's about being an adult and remaining a child, constantly amazed by the wonders of our multifaceted life.

The ancient Chinese philosopher Laozi once said that even a journey of a thousand miles begins with the first step.

And I hope that this book will help you take that step.

Good luck!

konstantin.kozhe@signatureaction.com

GOLF TERMINOLOGY DICTIONARY

Friends, golf is a whole world with its own language. In my book, there are many specialized golf terms. Here you can see what they mean.

Albatross - the number of strokes on a hole, three fewer than the par for that hole (on par-5 holes).

Amateur - a player not entitled to receive any monetary reward for their performances.

Bag - a case for clubs.

Birdie - the number of strokes on a hole, one fewer than par.

Bogey - the number of strokes on a hole, one more than par.

Break - a deliberately created slope on the green that causes the ball to deflect when struck.

Caddy - a player's assistant who is allowed to give advice during the game.

Chip - a low, short shot where the ball rolls a relatively long distance afterward; usually used when playing in close proximity to the green.

Cut - in major tournaments, the first two rounds serve as a kind of selection process, after which approximately half of the players are eliminated, losing the right to participate in the final two rounds and, consequently, the hope of winning, as well as (in professional tournaments) the opportunity to earn prizes.

Draw - a shot where the ball flies straight but slightly curves left at the end (for a player with a right-handed stance).

Drive - the first stroke on a hole, executed with a driver.

Driver - a club with the lowest angle of the head and the longest shaft.

Driving range - a separate area for practicing long shots.

Eagle - the number of strokes on a hole, two strokes less than par.

Fade - a shot where the ball flies straight but slightly curves to the right at the end (for a player with a right-handed stance).

Fairway - the area of medium-length grass occupying a significant part of the playing field between the tee and the green.

Flagstick - the flag placed in the hole so that players can see their ultimate target from a distance.

Flight - a group of players moving together on the course. A group can consist of two to four individuals.

Fringe - the area around the green, cut shorter than the fairway but longer than the green.

Golfer - a player in golf.

Green - the area with the shortest grass around the hole.

Handicap - a number indicating a golfer's skill level, calculated using a rather complex system and allowing for balancing the odds between beginners and experienced players.

Hole: 1) a single playing area from tee to green inclusive; 2) a depression in the green where the ball is putted.

Hook - a shot where the ball flies straight but significantly curves to the left afterward (for a player with a right-handed stance).

Hybrid - a club that combines characteristics of both a wood and an iron.

Iron - a club with a flat head.

Par - a standard norm used to calculate scores and assess players' levels. Par is the normative number of strokes a golfer should complete on a single hole or for the entire course during successful play.

Pitch - a not-so-long shot with a high trajectory, after which the ball hardly rolls; usually used when playing in close proximity to the green.

Professional - a professional player, tournament professional, or coach working in a golf club.

Putt - a rolling stroke made on the green.

Putter - a special club for the final rolling stroke.

Rough - an area of high grass, typically along the edges of the fairway.

Swing - the fundamental movement of a stroke using any club.

Score-card - a special card where game results are recorded.

Tee: 1) the area on the course from which play begins at each hole; 2) a wooden or plastic platform where a ball is allowed to be placed for the initial stroke at each hole.

Wood - a club with a large head, historically made of wood.

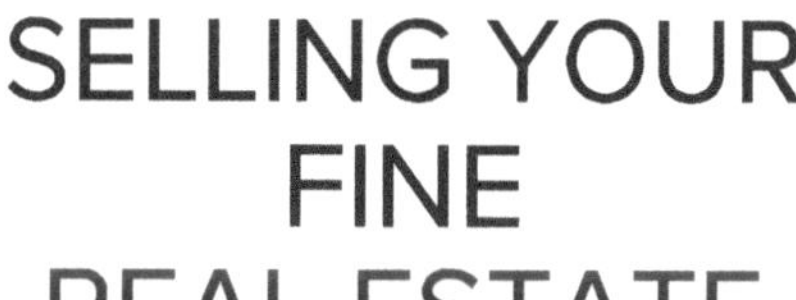

SIGNATURE ACTION | eXp REALTY

TRULY BORDERLESS

SELLING YOUR
FINE
REAL ESTATE

IN 6 WEEKS

AT THE MAXIMUM PRICE

RESIDENTIAL · COMMERCIAL · LUXURY

info@signatureaction.com   SPEAK WITH US TODAY   signatureaction.com

Five Spheres of Happiness

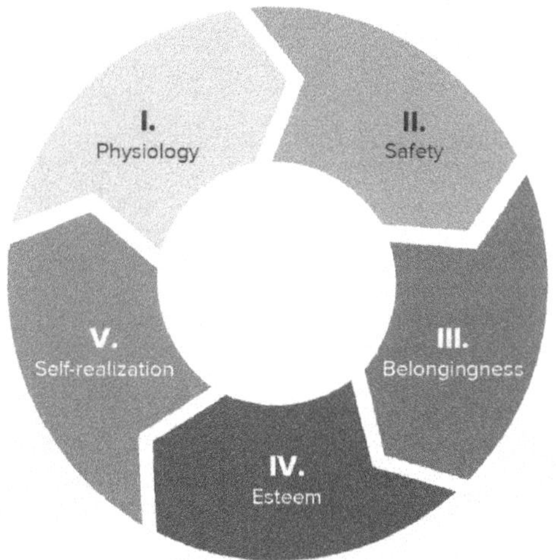

Testing according

TO DR. KONSTANTIN KOZHEVNIKOV'S

method

UNLOCK YOUR POTENTIAL
AND IDENTIFY AREAS OF GROWTH

kkmentorship.com

konstantin.kozhe.1mln.eng
signatureaction.com/mentorship
7-FUGURE STRATEGIC MENTORSHIP
Helping real estate professionals
realize their strategic potential, meet
life's challenges and achieve financial
success by creating the conditions for
sustainable growth and development
DR. KONSTANTIN KOZHEVNIKOV

EK ART.GALLERY

DIALOGUE WITH THE UNIVERSE
THOUGHTS AND FEELINGS
IN PAINT AND METAL

EXPRESSING COSMOS THROUGH FASHION`S LENS

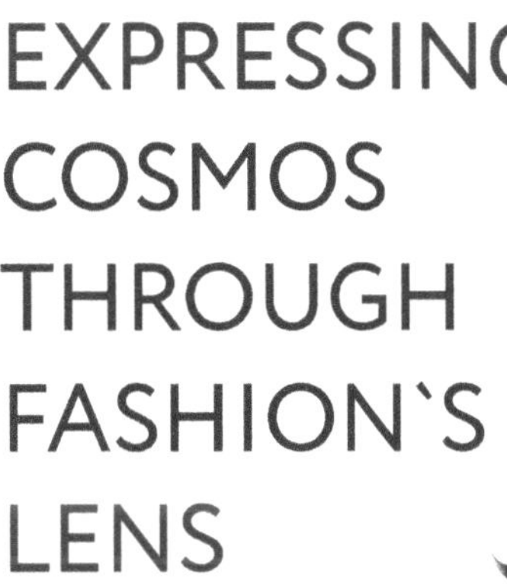

@EKART.GALLERY

@GALLERY.EK.ART

XENIADIDTHAT

INCLUSION-CONSCIOUS
PRO WRESTLING
JOURNALISM.
HOSTING &
BROADCASTING

XENIADIDTHAT.COM
@XENIADIDTHAT

XDT
MEDIA
STRATEGIC
MEDIA DEVELOPMENT
EDUCATION • BRAND IDENTITY • SOCIAL MEDIA • PUBLIC RELATIONS • & MORE
XENIADIDTHAT.COM
@XENIADIDTHAT

KONSTANTIN KOZHEVNIKOV

YOU CAN

BECOME YOUR OWN BEST FRIEND
AND BE HAPPY, HEALTHY AND WEALTHY

konstantin.kozhe@signatureaction.com

2024